ALSO BY GERRY VISCA:

IN STOCK AND AVAILABLE FOR PURCHASE WHILE QUANTITIES LAST

SO-BIZ-626

AVAILABLE AS A BOOK & 2 SET AUDIO CD
@ gerryvisca.com/hell
Comes with a gift of Why Time

I Don't Know What The Hell I'm Doing!®
Book and CD Audio Format

AVAILABLE AS A 3 PACK
@ gerryvisca.com/3pack
Comes with a gift of
Why Time

DEFYENEURS® Season 2
Inspiring Freedom

DEFYENEURS® Season 3
Live your WHY

Young DEFYENEURS®
Drive your Curiosity

AVAILABLE AS A BOOK
@ defyeneurs.com/season5

DEFYENEURS® Season 5
Inspired Athletes

THE FOLLOWING E-BOOKS ARE AVAILABLE NOW AS A FREE DOWNLOAD
- THE 50 MOST INSPIRED TIPS© @ gerryvisca.com/50tips
- BRAND U @ www.flipsnack.com or gerryvisca.com

AVAILABLE ON AMAZON
DEFYENEURS® Season 1
An Inspired Movement of Entrepreneurs

What Have You Got To Win? ®
The Success Principles to Winning Presentations

GET CREATIVE®
Unleash Your Creativity

THE INNOVATION GAP®
Cultivating Creativity in Life and Business

THINQ©
Live the Question

Dedicated to my little "Big Dreamer", Sophie.
You are a light in this world and your courage inspires me
everyday. You got this!

The observations, opinions, and comments within these stories DO NOT reflect those of the publisher; and in no way endorse any products or companies. The author and publisher have taken reasonable precautions in the preparation of this book and believe the facts presented in the book are accurate, as of the date it was written. However, neither the author nor the publisher assumes any responsibility for errors or omissions. The author and publisher specifically disclaim any liability resulting from the use or application of the information contained in this book. The information is not intended to serve as legal, financial, or other professional advice related to individual situations.

This publication is intended to provide general information regarding the subject matter covered. However, laws and practices often vary from state to state and are subject to change. As each factual situation is different, specific advice should be tailored to the particular circumstances. For this reason, the reader is advised to consult with his or her own advisor regarding their specific situation. For Photo Credits - please refer to the individual authors.

Defyeneurs® is a registered trademark of Redchair Branding Inc.
All rights reserved. No part of this publication may be used, reproduced, distributed, transmitted in any form or by any means, or stored in a database or retrieval system, without the prior written consent of the publisher.

Published by Redchair Branding Inc.
Hamilton, ON, Canada
www.gerryvisca.com
Copyright © 2016 by Redchair Branding Inc. and Gerry Visca

All rights reserved.
ISBN: 978-0-9939129-1-7

Written by Gerry Visca. First Edition - Season 1.
Art Direction by Redchair Branding Inc.
Edited by Angela Kontgen and Sara D'Arcey
Printed and bound in Canada

CONTENTS

Joe Griffin
©2000

FOREWORD
DAVID BYRD

Small things add up! We so often overlook the cumulative impact of the seemingly insignificant things in life. Life is a continuous series of seemingly small things that add up to equal the sum total of our worth as a part of humanity. Each of us represents one living soul, of great power, challenged with two choices: grow or decline. You must choose because there is no in-between position in life. For example, look at nature, everything in nature is either growing or decaying; there is no in-between. We are all part of this physical universe endued with great power that extends beyond the five senses. Some people intentionally choose the path of growth. However, most people unconsciously choose decline even though they are simply unaware that they have made any choice at all. They do so by accepting the limitations placed on them by the opinions of others or by their own limiting, self-imposed barriers of fear and doubtful beliefs. The path of abundance is a journey of growth, and that path is the one Big Dreamers choose.

This book is about Big Dreamers. I have a particular interest in all seven of these individuals, because I have had the unique privilege of working with and getting to know each of them very well. As the Founder and CEO of David Byrd Consulting LLC, I have invested over forty years of my career in the field of executive and leadership development. We specialize in next-level growth using a protocol that we refer to as the **Next Level Achievement System**™. In my career I have worked with thousands of Big Dreamers and have found that there is one characteristic that sets them apart. They hear and listen to their spirit rather than the noise of the crowd. They are not smarter, faster, more attractive or luckier than the rest, but they do have the capacity to go inside themselves and listen to their spirit - that inner voice that speaks with wisdom beyond conscious awareness. They generate a continuous, internal dialog of asking, seeking and knocking. They look for answers inside themselves simply because they know they are there. They trust that internal wisdom more than any external reality.

People often ask me if the choice of growth is easy or difficult. My answer is, neither. Being the only path to abundance, it is simply a choice. I find that when Big Dreamers make that choice, there is no turning back regardless of circumstances. It just is, whether easy or difficult.

All Big Dreamers reach a point in their journey where they find themselves at a crossroads. This is a self-defining moment. This moment may present itself once or multiple times along life's path. Some lose heart and quit because the current circumstances do not confirm success. The Big Dreamers, however, go within, listen to their spirit and ask a higher power for the strength to continue. Big Dreamers never look back and complain about their journey. In fact, listen as you read these stories, and you will hear relish! They take pride in their choices made and difficulties faced at each of life's crossroads. You will hear the relish of pride in the description of their choice of growth, regardless of circumstance at each defining moment. Gerry Visca has masterfully captured the very essence of the mind of Big Dreamers. His interview process and unique questioning ability pulled the very *guts* out of the mindset of these seven Big Dreamers. You, as I was, will be inspired by his descriptions of the heart and soul of real Big Dreamers.

Yes, our lives are composed of the sum total of our small choices and actions. We all travel the road of life, but in very different and specific ways. As you read these stories, you will be challenged with personal choices. Do I settle for normal, or do I choose to "march to the beat of a different drummer"? That alone makes this work of Gerry Visca significant.

Life poses two profound questions that stand before each of us at every moment. Do I make the choice to grow or decline? Make your choice because there is no in-between. Be challenged and inspired by Gerry Visca's insightful descriptions of these Big Dreamers!

David Byrd
Founder and CEO, David Byrd Consulting LLC

AUTHOR'S NOTE
GERRY VISCA
Why do you exist?

Big Dreamers

Why this book?

After launching *I Don't Know What The Hell I'm Doing!*®, it became clear to me that a large percentage of the world has stopped dreaming. For whatever reason, we just don't seem to dream big like we did years ago. We are living in the *Connection Age*, yet we are more disconnected than ever! It is one of the reasons I chose to start writing and publishing these inspiring books and blogs - to help people connect. My mission is to inspire 1 million *Why's* by connecting one another to what really matters most.

Why this topic?

I published an issue of *Defyeneurs*® themed, *Dream Again* a few years ago. It featured a cover story with Darin Kidd, of Lynchburg, Virginia, one of the stories featured in this book. It was this magazine issue that sparked my curiosity and inspired my intention to help the world dream bigger. On another note, it has become abundantly clear to me that for the first time in our history, obesity, terrorism, world hunger, eradication of our natural resources, global warming and economic depression are reaching epic levels. If we don't learn to continually innovate, collaborate and DREAM BIG, we won't be able to solve this growing global crisis. So, I hope this book will inspire all you dreamers out there to take action and DREAM BIG.

Why these Big Dreamers?

The *Defyeneurs*® issues I have published over the past 24 months, resonated with my vision to inspire a new ROI in the world - **R**each **O**ut and **I**nspire others. It was through writing these issues that I developed a deeper connection to these entrepreneurs I was interviewing. It allowed me glimpses into their inspiring journey and intrigued me. I wanted to uncover and ignite their full story. I didn't choose these authors as a result of their rank, status, or the company they are associated with, which is why; you will not see any corporations named in this book. I want the world to see THEM for who they truly are, in all their glory.

When developing the concept for this book, I set an intention to capture each person's journey in the most meaningful way possible. I spent hours personally interviewing each one of them and asking them dozens of thought-provoking questions. It was an emotional experience for them and for me. I feel privileged that each individual took the time and energy to collaborate with me on this project; and that they believed in my ability and desire to bring their story to life. This was the most intense undertaking of my publishing career and I feel very honoured for the opportunity. In publishing this book, I created two powerful intentions; the first was to extract the deeper realizations and insights from each one of their stories into 100 Dream Bits. The second, was to uncover and share their journey from a young age to the person they've become today. Within each of these interviews, I wanted to uncover the *shifts* that occurred to shape them into the Big Dreamers they are today. Although each of them has been published in other publications, this is the first time their full story has been explored in such depth. The architecture that shapes my style of publication includes a cross pollination of past and current projects. I find this type of interconnectivity helps bridge themes and brings them to life. In writing Big Dreamers, I integrated insights from my previous book, *I Don't Know What The Hell I'm Doing!®,* as frames for each chapter. I am overflowing with love and gratitude, for my life partner, Angela, and her continual support to my global vision. It's a true gift having someone you love witness your life mission. She has added to the richness of my inspirational work over these past 5 years, and so I thought it only fitting to have her write the introduction for this book. I am thrilled to have her energy in this book. I am also grateful to Jack Canfield, for recently publishing my story in his latest book titled, *Living the Success Principles®.* I'm thankful to David Byrd, for writing the foreword and sharing his extraordinary energy. He is a world-class leadership coach and has been an instrumental guide to each one of these Big Dreamer's lives.

What I know for certain is that there is a Big Dreamer living inside each one of us. It is time to ignite that fire within and start lighting up the world with your vision. So, close your eyes, have fun, and start dreaming big! With love and light,

Gerry Visca, Why Guy
Inspirational Speaker | Author | Publisher of Defyeneurs®

THE WORLD NEEDS BIG DREAMERS. CREATE WHAT YOU WANT MOST IN LIFE.

~ Gerry Visca

INTRODUCTION
Angela Kontgen
How will you live your one precious life?

Will you dare to wake up and step into your dreams or will you keep playing it safe and small until your life is over? It might sound a bit morbid to introduce a book this way, but we only have a brief time on this earth. I want this book to wake you up and allow you to start dreaming big! This book is full of inspiring stories from everyday dreamers – use it as your dream defibrillator. If you feel that you've put your own dreams on the back burner, this is the right book for you. I find there is nothing more amazing than inspiring someone to wake up and live his or her life. I love helping them follow their dream, before it is too late. So, I apologize if some of these words are a bit in your face, but I feel it's necessary to be so, as we've been asleep for far too long.

"Feel grateful to death for giving you another day, another experience, and for creating the scarcity that makes life so precious. If you do this, your life will no longer be yours to waste; it will be yours to appreciate."

~ Michael Singer, The Untethered Soul

Let's be honest, most of us take our lives for granted, as we never stop and really contemplate our limited time here. From about the age of 12, or for some of us, even earlier, we've turned off our dream machine and most of society ensures it remains shut down. I find this so tragic. For those of you who have children, don't you want them to pursue their dreams? Don't you think they need to see people they love and respect around them following their dreams? Don't you think it's time to change the scenario out there, wake up and do the work to ignite the dreamer inside of us?

Yes, you were born with a dream. You can sit there and shake your head and let your rational mind feed you *with rational lies* about how you are the only one who does not have a dream and does not know what it is. However, if you sit still long enough and just listen, somewhere inside you, your heart knows this is not true. The people on these pages are not made any different than you and I, so I hope you will find inspiration in their stories. I hope you can relate to each one of them and that this book will ignite the flame to uncover your own precious dream.

Allow each story to remove the barriers you have brilliantly put up, and reveal your own bigger, vibrant, living on my own terms life. All it takes in this moment is to set that intention. Know that holding this book, in this moment, is far from random. It's your decision here that counts – will you place this book on a shelf having barely skimmed the pages? Or will you allow it to ignite something inside of you?

It is through stories that we often find inspiration, because in stories we find pieces of ourselves. I know that you will relate to the challenges that each dreamer went through. You might be a single mom and can relate to the tenacity that Aana Camp went through to create a bigger life. Or perhaps, you once found yourself at absolute rock bottom and can relate to Danny Gasemy or Aaron Dinh's story. On the other hand, maybe you have tried many things like, Paddy McCracken or Brittany Burtz, so their stories will inspire you to keep going. Or perhaps you will be inspired at how Dale Munger went after his dreams, so that he could create a different legacy for his family. Whomever you relate to, there is no doubt that Darin Kidds' everyday energy, will inspire you to know that you've got it in you too.

I am also deeply grateful, that one of the best coaches I have ever met in my life, David Byrd, has written the foreword to this book. Thank you David, you inspire me to keep working on myself each day, so that I build the muscles to support my dreams.

Finally, this is all captured by one of the BIGGEST dreamers I know, Gerry Visca. His deeper driving Why is to inspire people and their ideas to action. He is on a mission to inspire 1 million Why's, so there is almost no better person to capture the stories of these Big Dreamers. He is a man who lives and breathes his dream, every single day. I've had the pleasure of witnessing the countless hours, and the heart and soul that Gerry has put into this dream, and I have loved seeing how inspired he has been by these extraordinary everyday dreamers. As he was conducting the interviews and devoting his energy to writing the chapters, I saw how moved to tears he was. Their stories are our stories. The details are perhaps a bit different, but they have all gone through the same struggles that seem to be a part of the human condition. They have walked the paths of doubt and fear. They have fallen and failed like all of us. The biggest difference is that they have fallen, perhaps even more than most of us, and simply picked themselves' up each time. If they can do it, you can too!

When professionals ask those on their deathbed, what they most regret in life, they never say that they regret not paying off their mortgage, or getting that promotion, or another big screen TV. What they all say, is that they regret not "going for it." They all regretted not going after their dreams. Life is precious; so don't waste another single drop of it. Your dreams are waiting for you - they never go away. You were born whole and complete and with a dream in your soul, now let's ignite that baby shall we?

Like anything Gerry writes and publishes, you will come to see this book has a great energy about it. You will want to walk around with it – stop and read a story when you are feeling off track or like you can't go on anymore. Perhaps, you will do one of the cool exercises, Gerry has provided and it will jolt you to take action on your life. So, grab the pages of this book like your life depends on it - because it does. Have a notebook and pen beside you for those moments you feel inspired, because I guarantee you something inside of you will come to life again when you read this book.

Angela Kontgen
Meditation & Mindset Coach | Editor of Defyeneurs®

The Top 20 Actions People Don't Take.

1. I don't work on myself everyday.

2. I don't take physical care of myself.

3. I don't read or listen to something inspiring everyday.

4. I don't meditate or visualize my dreams.

5. I don't create and share my affirmations out loud.

6. I don't surround myself with other big dreamers.

7. I don't decide on what I want most.

8. I don't create my own way. Instead I follow others.

9. I don't say NO to the distractions. I say YES to everyone.

10. I don't choose love. I choose to remain in fear.

11. I don't create a plan of goals or monthly milestones.

12. I don't seek out advice from experts.

13. I don't focus on creating a new story.

14. I don't take daily action.

15. I don't carve out the time to live the RIGHT actions.

16. I don't create dream or vision boards.

17. I don't attend any inspiring events.

18. I don't prioritize my time.

19. I don't ask for help. Instead I do everything myself.

20. I don't get enough rest.

The Top 20 Limiting Beliefs to Dreaming Big.

1. I don't have enough money.
2. I don't have the education.
3. I'm not smart enough.
4. I haven't done it before.
5. No one will support my vision.
6. I don't know enough people.
7. I might fail.
8. My family won't support me.
9. I'm too old or I'm to young.
10. I don't have the time.
11. It will take too long, to create my vision.
12. I have too many negative people in my life.
13. I'm not trained or certified.
14. I was raised in a negative environment.
15. No one will want my idea.
16. I don't have enough Face Book friends or likes.
17. There is too much competition.
18. I don't know HOW to do it, so I can't start.
19. I have to keep it a secret my from spouse.
20. I have burned too many bridges, so no one will support me.

1. Danny Gasemy

<u>WHAT</u> do you want?

"Nothing is more rewarding than building relationships, sharing your experiences, and influencing others to succeed." Danny Gasemy

Danny Gasemy *exists* to better people's lives. It's a beautiful May 19th afternoon, the day before Danny's 47th birthday and I can still feel my anticipation as I call this extraordinary Big Dreamer. I first interviewed Danny for my publication, *Defyeneurs®*, *The Top 50 Relationship Marketing Tips* issue, in December 2015. He has served so many people and I feel such an inspiring connection to this, now, Hawaiian settler. I greeted Danny by saying, "Aloha", one of the few Hawaiian words I know. He moved to this majestic part of the world just three short days ago, and for the past three days, he has been taking in all of the details of this newfound paradise. Even before starting our interview, I'm reminded of a great mentor, the late Dr. Wayne Dwyer, who left everything, including his shoes, to move to Hawaii and live out his life as one of the greatest self-help authors and teachers of all time. I admire people that don't wait for someday to step into their lives and Danny has done just that.

It's the last interview of the week; I'm mentally exhausted, yet after hearing Danny's first few words, I'm immediately bustling with inspiration. Danny begins to answer my first question and is instantly overcome with great emotion. I had asked him to share his childhood experience with me. He responded, "I just got chills thinking about it." Danny grew up in a beautiful 10,000 square foot home, in what he terms, the Beverly Hills of Maryland. His father was a successful doctor, driven in everything he pursued; yet, he was quite frugal with Danny. Unlike his neighbourhood friends, he had to pay his own way through college. His father instilled strong values of working for money. Nothing was ever handed down to Danny.

He reflects on how his sister, was recently helping their parents, sort through some old boxes held in storage. Inside one of the boxes, was a high school graduation photo of Danny and his guidance councillor. "The funny part of this photo, was my parents jumping for joy in the background," he recounted. Danny had a learning disability and really struggled in high school. After relocating from a private school, he was held back in the 10th grade and just barely graduated. Unlike his friends, who knew where they were going, he was unsure of his next steps and felt a sense of hopelessness upon graduation.

As all of his friends made their way to college, funded by their parents, Danny chose to work at a nearby deli. He was desperately trying to save up for his tuition and eventually, after raising the funds; Danny attended college to study physical therapy. The only way he could afford to go to College though was by driving back home, every weekend, to work double shifts at the deli. It was a long

Big Dreamers

and difficult journey - saving money and working numerous jobs. Nothing ever came easy to him during those years.

The drive back and forth from college to the deli, took its toll on him. "I kept asking myself, what am I doing and what do I really want?" He was uncertain as to where this path was going to lead him and after attending college for a couple of years; he was baffled to learn that practicing as a physical therapist required a master's degree. One thing he knew for certain was that he disparaged the idea of staying in college for another 4 years!

Danny chose to quit college in his senior year. Upon reflection, years later, he feels a sense of regret for not completing his degree knowing full well he could have. It was this decision that led him to the world of construction however, and he remained there for the next seven years.

Now in his late 20's, he was frustrated and disconnected from his future path. Danny would sometimes work 14-hour days in construction. The long and arduous hours intensified his desire to one day create his own business. "If I was going to pour that many hours into working for others, I would rather build my own dream," he shares. He often shared with his friends, his passion for being an entrepreneur. Sadly, they discouraged him from leaving the work force. "They didn't think I had what it took to be an entrepreneur."

Knowing that something had to change, Danny decided to make the transition from residential to corporate construction. His hard work ethic seemed to pay off at first. He was promoted to senior estimator and then vice president of business development. He was even upgraded to a larger 20' x 20' office. To the outside world, he was a success, but inside, he was completely unfulfilled with his life. He hated not owning his own time. His daily routine consisted of a two-hour commute and essentially had him living at the construction office. He was always the first employee to check in and the last to turn off the lights. "I used to stare out the window of my office and ask myself, is this what I really want to do with my life?"

Working at the deli, he used to daydream of being successful. He spent a lot time getting to know highly successful people and that fuelled his desire for a more purposeful life. He acknowledges that he participated in every decision of his life up to this point, yet he believed he was meant for more. Meanwhile, back at the corporate construction office, Danny's patience with management was running thin. The event that finally tipped the scale was when his boss yelled at him for being 15 minutes late. "That was it. The last thing I needed or deserved was to have this man yell at me, especially after working my ass off. I felt like a rebel and decided to show up the next day wearing a t-shirt, jeans and no shoes," he recounts. He had enough and he lavished at the idea of owning his own time. He embraced a new mindset, that no one had the right to own his time. He had a strong work ethic, which had helped earn millions of dollars for this company, so the last thing he wanted was to be treated so poorly.

Looking back, he is able to see these work experiences as a gift, which taught him the value of his time. He knew he was a hard worker and he was eager to learn the skills that would enable him to progress in his job, but he wouldn't stand for being poorly treated or spoken to. Even though he felt unsure, as to the direction he was heading in life, he knew he was a Big Dreamer with big ambitions.

These kinds of confrontations ignited a fire inside of him and pushed him to dream even bigger. This was a consistent and common thread, which weaved throughout his late 20's - a desire to create and live his life on his terms.

The successful customers that frequented the deli where Danny worked in his early years were shimmering stars. He was always drawn to the most successful customers. He used his encounters with them as an opportunity to ask them questions about their path to success. He became a sponge, absorbing all their wisdom and knowledge - he could not get enough! Every conversation intensified and fuelled his fire and desire for success. Visions of working for himself and controlling his own hours filled him with tremendous joy. What seemed like a rebellious executive in the corporate construction office was actually a young and proud man standing up for himself. He was telling the world he was meant for more and that no one had the right to own his time.

As he approached the age of 31, he was ready to create a new chapter and kick-start his entrepreneurial journey. It took him 18 months to summon the courage to leave the construction industry for a new career in network marketing. All of his friends and family criticised his decision. They predicted he would fail as an entrepreneur and pleaded with him to abandon such a wild idea at this stage of his life. He was a senior executive in a successful corporate construction office. "My friends would ask me why I wanted to leave the comfort of an office job - they just didn't get me. They thought I had fallen off the reservation and was in need of an intervention," he remembers. His friends tried to do whatever they could to discourage him from pursuing one of those so-called, "pyramid schemes". He had invested significant time and energy, building someone else's dream. He had witnessed for too many years his bosses coming and going when they felt like it and taking exotic vacations. This was the lifestyle he dreamed of living. He was a Big Dreamer and he dreamed of controlling his own time. He had enough of being told what to do and when he could do it! He had reached his boiling point, learning that hard work alone wasn't enough and, for him, only resulted in insignificant salary increases. For so many years, he had poured himself into this way of being and he wasn't getting ahead or any younger. He was ready to challenge himself and the status quo. He was ready for more and to take control of his own destiny, to see his own dreams realized.

Danny was 31 and living in his hometown of Maryland. For the next 11 years, he would find himself working even harder than ever before on his own network marketing business. Days flowed into nights and he often found himself forgetting what day it was. He struggled, but it didn't matter to him, he was his own boss and finally calling the shots. After 11 years of slaving away, building up his business and sponsoring well over 500 people into his company, it just didn't seem to have an impact on his success. Despite his incredible work ethic as a lead trainer, delivering web-based training for the entire company, his efforts just didn't match up with his dream of financial freedom. He was trying to do everything to fuel his success. He was managing all of the weekly meetings, monthly regional training for the area, and even administrating their back office.

In the meantime, one of Danny's best friends had moved to California and was continually sharing photos with him. He encouraged him to relocate to this sunny paradise and in 2005, at the age of 35, Danny did. He sold two of his houses, packed up all of his belongings and made the trek to Laguna Beach, California. Leaving the only home he knew, he found himself being pulled by a stronger energy. As I enthusiastically listen to Danny speak, I recall a scene from the movie *Jerry McGuire*, starring Tom Cruise, as he drives and sings at the top of his lungs the famous Tom Petty song, *Free Fallin*. I can't help but draw similarities and picture Danny doing the same thing on his drive out to sunny California.

It was now March 1, 2005 and Danny was bustling harder than ever to drive his life forward. He had the pedal to the metal and was looking out the windshield at his new life waiting to receive him. He kept reminding himself that he was a Big Dreamer. He had the courage to leap out of his comfort zone, a quality that he fondly remembers from the many success stories those successful people would share with him while working at the deli. Nothing would stop him now.

Paradise awaited his arrival, or so he thought! For the next 6 months, his best friend with the "big opportunity" set him up in a bottom bunk bed, with his 18-year-old brother-in-law sleeping above him in a dark and tiny room. While laying there looking up at the underside of the bed, listening to the snoring sounds, he once again questioned his existence. "All I could think of was, 'what the hell am I doing living here?' The next day, I moved out into my own house, up the street". He had officially changed his postal code from

Maryland to sunny Laguna Beach, California. Despite his sunny and sandy surroundings, Danny felt that all his hard work in network marketing was beginning to feel like quick sand. He was struggling harder than ever before. He could barely pay his rent, and there never seemed to be any food in his fridge. Friends were continually giving him handouts. "It was a really tough time. I was forced to get food from the church, as I just couldn't seem to stand on my own", he shares. Roommates would come and go and the hours he dedicated to his business seemed to increase to 60 plus hours a week. Danny was grabbing whatever little handyman jobs his friends would throw his way just to stay afloat. Life seemed bleak and once again, he felt hopeless and unsure of his future.

At the age of 35, while sitting in his home in Laguna Beach, depression and sadness started kicking in fast and furiously. He was spiralling downward with little hope in sight. He had reached the lowest point in his life and he knew it. He shut himself off from society and began isolating himself, in what his friends called, "the cave". His surroundings and attitude towards life were magnifying his depression. In his mind, he wished and hoped for more, but everything around him contradicted what he was visualizing. "Sitting there in the darkness, I didn't feel I had a way out. Then, I remember being on my couch, and suddenly, I was inspired to paint and create something". He didn't know where this feeling was emanating from, but he knew he had to pour his feelings onto a canvas. Scrambling around to find whatever change he could find, he quickly gathered up a few dollars and bolted out to a nearby art supply store, where he purchased a small set of paints and a canvas.

Big Dreamers

"I couldn't wait to get back home and start splashing paint on the canvas," he shares. He was suddenly inspired and after a few hours of existing in this state of a creative frenzy, he stopped to view his painting of a beautiful woman. "Well, that was my intention, however, the end result ended up resembling the head of Medusa," he recalls with laughter. That didn't stop him from pursuing his newfound passion though. He even called his sister and shared his intensity and desire to create with her. He needed more canvases and he needed them fast! He could not afford to buy any more canvases, so he decided to build his own frames. He drove over to Home Depot and grabbed as much of their scrap pieces of wood as they would let him. He then searched on Craig's List to find an economical source for canvas, where he found a 75-foot roll of material for a bargain. He began to build his own canvases and for the next 2 years, he poured his passion into creating 70 paintings. He found a creative outlet to channel his depression and despair. This creative action ignited the Big Dreamer inside of him again and he was becoming a new man.

Painting became his positive outlook and metaphor for creating his desired life. He mastered the art of building his own frames and stretching his own canvasses. His appreciation for colour and light seemed to illuminate his soul. He learned that he could overcome the feelings of despair by channelling his thoughts into positive action and directing the noise in his head onto canvas. This was a major transformation in his life, as he became the architect of his thoughts and the designer to a new reality.

For the first time in his life, Danny felt he was in control. He was not going to sit on his couch wallowing in sadness any longer. His daily routine, consisted of working long 12-hour days on his business, returning home at 10:00 p.m. and paint until 3:00 a.m. in the morning. Eventually, this new passion started generating revenue and it kept Danny alive. He was on fire and went on to create furniture, mosaics, and many more paintings. "My buddies thought I was crazy, but I didn't care. I found a way to survive and pull myself out of depression." Danny had cultivated a new mindset of positivity and a new outlook on his future. He learned how to block out the negative feedback around him and take control of his life. This creative expression became a powerful outlet, which transformed his frustration into feelings of infinite possibility.

~ Dream Bit ~
Big Dreamers Attract The Way

Big Dreamers don't wait for others to validate their choices. They don't live their life by what others think. There is a new type of success emanating inside of them and they learn how to master their minds by attracting creative ways to fuel their success.

As this new passion started to take hold, Danny converted his living room into a lively art studio. He got rid of his pool table and laid out plastic sheets along the living room floor and half way up the walls. He cared very little about what others thought and became impervious to their negative feedback. His stretched canvases became his super hero cape and the wooden frames the foundation as he started to build his dreams. His brushes were his new tools for success and with every stroke and splash of colour he overcame his adversity. The areas of his life that used to feel like dark shadows were now replaced with colour, light, and endless possibility. Every nook and cranny in his home was filled with beautiful paintings and new possibilities.

Danny finally started to feel like a Big Dreamer. His creative outlet became an instrument for downloading his emotions onto paper. This is a powerful success strategy used by any top leader. "So many people suffer, by keeping emotional baggage in their heads and trying to process it." When you keep it trapped inside the garbage builds up to the point where your mind is weighing you down. The key is to take out the trash and empty the thousands of thoughts that pass through your mind on a daily basis. In some of the darkest moments in his life, Danny taught himself to master this art of taking out the trash in his mind and created something beautiful with it. Ironically enough, his friends who used to be his biggest critics started admiring his work and began requesting customized pieces for their homes.

29

~ Dream Bit ~
Big Dreamers Convert Fear Into Love

Big Dreamers convert fear into love. They understand the only power they have over their circumstances is the way in which they respond. They don't let their emotions control them for they know that they can control the energy through creative outlets.

Despite his creative breakthrough, life continued to challenge Danny. His family was now in financial distress and his parents were on the verge of losing his childhood home. Danny didn't have the financial means, at this stage, to even fly home and help them move. He started to feel powerless in his inability to support himself and his family in need. For months, he couldn't even afford gas for his car. "I never knew what it felt like to actually fill up a tank of gas so instead, I would use whatever change I was able to scrape up, just to make it to the next stop," he recounted. His gas needle never made it past a 1/8th of a tank. Gasoline wasn't the only fuel he was running out of, his energy was quickly on the verge of reaching empty. Personal loans were accumulating and rapidly ramping up to $30K of debt. Close friends were feeding him on a regular basis and he had no idea how he would pay them back. It was at that time when his best friend, Mark, called him up and shared an exciting new opportunity to sell skin care in the anti-aging industry. "I dropped the phone and couldn't believe my ears. I have no money, no ability to pay my bills; I am barely surviving and my friend wants me to join him in a new network marketing company selling skin care!"

Danny didn't feel as if he had the energy in him to start again, in yet another network marketing company. He was actually working up the courage to ask his friend, Mark for another $500 loan, so he could fly home and help his parents. Danny had even contemplated putting his dreams on hold and returning to the construction industry, to pay off his debts. He was doing whatever he could to pay his rent and even took up an offer from his friend to paint his home in Hawaii, in exchange for a month of rent. He hit rock bottom and the last thing on his mind was starting out on a new venture in an industry he knew nothing about. Sitting there on his couch listening to his friend, he couldn't believe that 11 years has passed by and this was the life he had to show for it. His original idea, was to come out to California for a year, to spend with his friend, building his first network marketing company. "I'm 42 years old and all I could think was, 'where did the time go?'" Aside from a house filled with paintings and memories of helping a friend renovate his home in Hawaii, a distraught Danny, felt he had accomplished very little in his life.

The turning point of his life began in September of 2011, when he decided to meet up with the founder of this new anti-aging company. "He helped me believe I could build anything that I set my mind to. I had learned how to build houses, so I could learn to build my dreams," he recounted. He later noted, "I remember him asking me to invest the next 5 years of my life, towards building this opportunity and it would pay off 10 fold." Something resonated with the words he heard. Somehow, he believed, this was the way and the opportunity to transform his life and the lives of his struggling family.

So once again, Danny found himself at a crossroads. Would he ask his friend to loan him money to fly home and take a job in construction, or would he join this new network marketing company in an industry he had no experience in? "Where would I find the money and the energy to pursue this new opportunity? At the time, I didn't know if I had it in me," he recalls. He was already feeling defeated, so how would he attract success in this new venture? Like all Big Dreamer's though, his belief in himself, attracted something bigger. He had learned how to displace the fear and the rational thinking in his mind. The founder had sparked an inner feeling and belief in this new anti-aging company. Danny was opening up to this opportunity and suddenly experiencing a surge of excitement. He recalls this feeling like it was yesterday, "I remember sitting there, looking at the founder in the eyes and suddenly feeling that I had nothing to lose." He saw his friend Mark walk away from everything to start at the bottom with this new company. Danny knew in his heart this was an opportunity he couldn't pass up. He was 100% in and ready to begin moving forward with this new chapter of his life.

He immediately put his used VW Jetta on Craig's List and sold it to the first person that showed up. A wave of tears suddenly ran down his cheeks, as he shared the events that followed next. He called his mom and when she answered, he gave her the power to choose his next steps. "I was prepared to fly home and help them move out of our family home or stay in California and build this new business, for them. My mom tearfully responded, Danny, you stay there and build this business son." So, on September 17th, 2011, he made a commitment to himself, that he was going to build this new business and visit his family, once a month, no matter where he was in the world. He has never broken that promise and continues to this day to visit them monthly.

When you ask him what drives his daily actions and his ability to dream bigger, he confidently responds, that it's his parents. He finally arrived at a point in his life, where he can truly help his parents. He recently treated them all to a paid vacation to Hawaii. His family means the world to him. "The luxuries don't mean anything to me. When I visit my parents in their new townhouse in Maryland, my mom sets up a small kids bed for me in the dining room." All that matters to him is that he is with his family.

Danny had to face a pool of challenges on his path to success. Every month he faced the uncertainty of whether he would have enough money to pay the monthly rent. He lived off the handouts from his friends and received food from the church. He invested 11 years of his life trying to build a network marketing business with very little success. He had an enormous debt that he didn't know how he would pay off. So, as he laid in his mother's dining room, all he could do was give thanks to God for the life he had created. He views his life journey as a beautiful orchestration of events, which led him to the place where he now lives. It is a life of love, friendship, family, great abundance, peace and freedom. He is a Big Dreamer and now teaches and motivates others around him to do the same. "I share the same message with everyone - never give up on your dream and stick to your vision, it's the only thing that will pull you out of hell."

Within the first 17 days of joining his new business, he had already accelerated through the first 3 ranks. He fondly remembers qualifying for the company's car bonus and couldn't believe it was real. Danny and his friends went to pick up his new car on Halloween night in 2011. He vividly remembers the feeling of sitting in the dealership, sweating with anxiety for fear of not being approved for the lease payments. To Danny's surprise, the dealership approved his application to lease the new car. The first thing he did once leaving the dealership was call his company's headquarters, he needed reassurance that this car bonus was for real. He knew how bleak his credit rating was, as a result of the past 11 years of scrambling to make ends meat. The last thing he wanted to worry about was having the pressure of assuming monthly car lease payments on a brand new car. It had only been a few short weeks ago, that he had sold his VW Jetta for $3,200, so he could make this work. He patiently waited for someone at the corporate headquarters to answer the phone, and more importantly, to provide him with the reassurance that this car bonus was the real deal. "I'll never forget the words that echoed through my ears as the phone operator confidently replied, "yes, your car bonus is for real," he recounted. He ended the call, placed his phone in his pocket and immediately fell to his knees. For the next hour, he sat on the side of the road staring at the brand new white Lexus. "Suddenly, I couldn't wait to help so many other people, experience this joyous feeling." He was elated and filled with tremendous gratitude, for he could feel his life finally getting on track. He knew how to dream big, and he finally found a way to make his years of dreaming a reality.

With his hands gripping the soft leather steering wheel, he was ready to travel a new road of prosperity and growth. He was fired up and wanted to help the next dozen or so people on his team qualify for their car bonus. He had just proven to himself, and to others around him, he could do anything he set his mind to; and the view suddenly never looked so clear. The horizon gave him a sense of comfort and he knew he was finally in the right place, at the right time. He was confident in his gift to help his parents experience new levels of financial freedom too. He knew he found his purpose in life and an inspired way to help the masses. Had any of his life events not occurred as they did, he would not be in this place ready to soar like an eagle. As he accelerated his new car, he felt a surge of energy coursing through his veins. He opened all of the windows and in that moment, they resembled his new windows of opportunity. All he had to do was look up and out. He was inspired to unwrap the gift that God had given to him. He was now on an exalted mission; to help others drive their success. He had the GPS of dreaming bigger in hand and he finally knew where he was heading. Nothing could stop him, as he was on the open road with a new company and limitless opportunities.

Now in his 47th year, he is having fun and driving his success. For the past 4 and half years, he has travelled 3 times a week, all across the globe. Time has taken on a whole new meaning. "I love how I make time to enjoy the simple pleasures of life with family and friends," he shares. Throughout his past few weeks of travel he managed to visit his home in Maryland, while checking in on the details of a new house he is building. He got to enjoy fresh lobster in Maine, and attended his uncle's 80th birthday in Connecticut. Many of Danny's colleagues, often criticise him for how hard he appears to be working. "I'm having the time of my life, travelling and seeing the world, it's my new office." It has given him the time, money, and freedom, to finally experience the wonders of life.

For Danny, it's not enough to simply visualize his dream, but to actually taste, savour, and experience it in every detail. This way of living speaks to his soul. His dream and vision was ignited years ago, while serving and conversing with the successful people in the deli, but now he is the one being served. He is the one giving advice to the next generation of Big Dreamers.

I asked him to picture himself getting into a time machine and paying his younger self a visit at the deli, "what advice would he offer to a younger Danny?" Taking a moment to ponder this question, he was once again, overcome with great emotion. It was as if he was actually in the moment, visiting a younger version of himself and time suddenly felt like an illusion. "I would tell myself to never, ever, give up on your dreams, and break away from the friends that are holding you down. To surround yourself with people that believe in you."

~ Dream Bit ~
Big Dreamers Create New Associations

The world is filled with people that won't support your dreams, and they exist for a reason, to remind you of what you are meant to be. Big Dreamers tap into a new and inspired energy, that once released, attracts new and positive people into their lives.

For Danny, his unsupportive friends became the energy source he needed to help break away and propel upward. He never cut ties, only respected their opinions. He chose not to buy into their opinions, but he would save all of the private messages encouraging him to give up on his dream of a network marketing company, and to pursue a safer and conservative route. Today, these ankle biters are now his greatest cheerleaders. "Now my friends tell me they always knew I had it in me, and how they always believed in my vision".

We need to seek out people that won't let us play small. We need to surround ourselves with people that reinforce and encourage us, as we pursue our dreams. Recently, Danny's grade ten teacher posted a special comment on social media, sharing his admiration and respect for Danny and even encouraged him to share his story to his class. This really touched Danny, as he shares, "The belief that my teacher instilled within me, has stayed with me all these years."

He continued to reminisce, about the girlfriend he had planned to marry in high school, and how her parents were unwilling to give him their blessing, as a result of his reluctance to pursue a college degree. He still feels the pain those words inflicted in his heart. "It was hard hearing those words. They couldn't let their daughter be with someone they believed wouldn't amount to anything," he recounted.

~ Dream Bit ~
Big Dreamers Shape Their Destiny

When Big Dreamers feel isolated from the world they choose to go deeper. They choose to feel their dream. It is in the moments when no one seems to be supporting their vision, that they shape their destiny.

They choose to listen to their inner voice and master their life.

It's during those challenging moments that Danny chose to see a different reality, than what others saw for him. He believed in his heart that he was successful, and that he would one day live a successful life. "Without a deeper belief in yourself, you won't have the power to push above and beyond the people that want to hold you down." It's that inner belief that creates a shield to protect your dream.

What was the shift that Danny experienced years ago, that made him take 100% responsibility for living his dreams? He recalls being at his house with no food in the fridge. He rustled through all of the drawers and cupboards, and to his surprise he managed to find one good can of French cut beans. "Is this what my life has come to, one can of beans?" he reflects. He was hungry, but not beaten down, and somehow, not defeated. After eating this last bit of food, he looked up and started coaching himself. "I told myself, I'm a fighter, I'm coachable and I'm a dreamer." These were the words that became the catalyst, and the shift for a new existence.

The opportunity in the anti-aging industry, which was an industry that never entered this conscious, would change the course of his life forever. "When my friend Mark first shared the opportunity with me, I thought it was a sick joke." Trusting in his friend and the energy of something bigger propelled him into action and he tirelessly shares the opportunity with everyone he encounters. In those first few weeks, he and his growing team, were inspired to build awareness for what they believed would become the biggest thing in the industry. It wasn't unusual for him to work from 8:00 a.m. to midnight, every day. He knew he was given an opportunity of a lifetime though, and he chose to make the most of it.

For the first three months, he had no clue what the hell he was doing, but he always knew why; to help his parents experience financial freedom. He would do whatever had to be done, including putting over 38,000 miles on his new car, within the first 18 months of running his new business. He was so exhausted from long days of driving and sharing, that he would find himself falling asleep during conversations. He was tired, but at the same time, never felt more alive. He was driven with a newfound purpose, to share his passion and enthusiasm with as many people as he could get to listen. He never looked up to question whether his efforts were resulting in sales.

Days quickly rolled into nights, as he and his team, shared this amazing opportunity with others. When he experienced rejection, he closed his eyes and fixated on the vision of being close to his family. He felt the feeling of making a profound impact on their financial future. Family and friends are Danny's oxygen source. He was now driven with a new form of energy that fuelled his daily actions. He was an unstoppable force. Flashes of his past interactions with the most successful people in the deli, merged onto his vision board. He saw himself, travelling the world with his friends, and experiencing a new kind of freedom. He knew that his happiness would precede, and drive his success. His years of sticking to his dreams, created a massive root system below the surface, that would one day, spawn a bountiful harvest.

It was his unwavering inner belief that attracted him to this global opportunity. Some would say it was a matter of being at the right place at the right time. However, the most successful people have shared that you have to be ready and open to seizing these opportunities when they appear in your life.

I love Danny's no nonsense attitude, when it comes to helping his team experience the same form of success. "Once I uncover someone's reason for doing this business, whether it be for their family, their kids, or a better lifestyle, I will always throw it back in front of them." He has come to the realization that sugar coating a situation doesn't necessarily help someone move forward. "A lot of people ask me for the "nice Danny" during a tough situation, knowing full well that what they really need is a dose of the "honest Danny."

I also love how real Danny is, and the life of simplicity he lives. He smiles and laughs, when discussing how he prefers to shop at thrift stores. Even though he is living financially free, it's important to him to be real. The driving force for Danny is the experiences he can create with his friends and family. This Big Dreamer is a real, genuine, authentic man; with a heart of gold that will help anyone that needs him. It is this energy that attracts me to shine a light on his story. It's his drive, persistence, belief in himself, and his willingness to help all those around him, that compels me to share his story, and his energy with the world.

He prescribed his own medicine and wrote the prescription for his own success. In the earliest days of building his new business, he even wrote on his office white board a declaration that would change his life. Danny explains, "If I didn't follow through on my actions, then I instantly had to call my Dad and tell him, I was giving up on him and mom, and they were on their own." To move himself and his vision forward, he created a personal mastery system. He gave himself 15 seconds to phone someone else on his list after receiving a rejection. What made this system so effective was his commitment to the alternative. If he didn't follow through with making that second call, then he would be forced to call his Dad. He proved to himself that he was willing to go the extra mile everyday for his family.

~ Dream Bit ~

Big Dreamers Declare Their Intentions With Purpose

Big Dreamers are willing to fail by embracing rejection as part of the journey. They master the ability to overcome disappointment and they don't let it derail their efforts. They continually raise the bar and hold themselves accountable to a higher personal standard.

"Four and half years later, I've never made that call to my Dad," he shares. Even though, Danny has exceeded his financial goals, he still holds himself accountable by living the declaration that is still written on his white board.

Listening to Danny share his story and his insights, I'm reminded why I'm so passionate about my previous book called, *I Don't Know What the Hell I'm Doing®!* As he set out on his new venture, he never knew what the hell he was doing, but he was driven by a deeper *Why* to change his parent's lives.

"Ready, Fire, Aim"! This quote from my colleague and mentor, Jack Canfield, author of *The Success Principles®,* sums up Danny's extraordinary life experience. Every part of his journey has been an opportunity to refine his approach. Every crossroads presented him with choices. The way he responded either advanced him forward or placed him in reverse. All of us have the choice to change the course of our lives every single day. We all live on the same planet, governed by the same laws of attraction. Each one of us is faced with challenges and choices. The bigger the challenge, the bigger the opportunity you are pursuing. When we start to embrace challenge as an opportunity for growth, we disrupt the status quo and define our lives. When we commit to replacing years of poorly conditioned habits with new successful ones, we change our attitude and influence new behaviours.

~ Dream Bit ~

Big Dreamers Do The Inner Work On Themselves

Big Dreamers are focused on changing the only thing they have the power to control - themselves. They do the inner-work everyday, not just when it's all sunshine and roses, but during the dark and cloudy times. They get their feelings and emotions out of their heads and onto paper. They define the outcomes that they wish to experience.

He created his life, by choosing to take 100% responsibility for the life he intended to create. He stumbled and fell the first few months in his new anti-aging business, yet he persevered, by continually sharing the opportunity. After months of sharing, the right people appeared, and more importantly, listened. His perseverance started paying off through small and daily wins. He climbed the ranks, faster and faster, gaining tremendous momentum. He called his Dad and flew him and his mom, out to the company's first convention. He was proud to share the success he achieved, and show them the man he had become.

Danny's Top Actions for Dreaming Bigger:

Create the master life list. No matter what business you're in, create on paper; the biggest master life list possible. Don't stop at the first 20 to 30 names. Think back, to every person you've ever known, even from the earliest age, including elementary school right through to college. Think about every place you've lived and worked in. Expanding your mind will help you create your master list. Even though Danny had worked in this business for 16 years, he never created this kind of master life list. This unique strategy jump-started his success. "If 90 people on your list of 100 said no, would you call the final 10? Most people wouldn't, and that is what separates successful people from unsuccessful people." Successful people are simply driven to look foolish, fail, fail again and eventually, fail better. "What if I was number 91 on your list, would you call me, knowing that I was just a construction worker?"

Don't pre-judge the people on your list. Big Dreamers know that some people will jump on board and some, for whatever reason, just won't. It is important to remember that there is always someone on your list waiting for an opportunity.

Don't take it personally. Take control of your emotions and your reaction to the rejections you will receive. Remove yourself from the outcome and limit your expectations. Share the opportunity with enthusiasm and passion, by leading with your driving Why. Whatever you do, don't burn any bridges. "Imagine attracting that 91st person on your list of 100, and years later, you changed the direction of their family's financial future forever."

Embrace new levels of empathy. Realize that most people are not going to think like you. As a leader, you have to embrace new levels of empathy for where people are at in their lives. Most people aren't driven for change and success as you are. The goal is to meet and lead people where they are in the present moment. Some people need to crawl, others jog, and a few will run like the wind.

Get obsessed with where you want to be. The most successful people on the planet share a common denominator, a relentless pursuit to realize their dreams. To reach your dreams, you'll need to become bullet proof. You will need to strengthen the quality of your mind through ongoing personal development. Big Dreamers commit to serious change. They close themselves off to distractions and make time for what really matters. For things to truly change, you have to be willing to change your life. Developing yourself personally includes immersing yourself with positive materials such as: self-help books and self-help audio programs, uplifting monthly events, and weekly coaching.

Say no to the naysayers and yes to your dreams. When you commit to displacing the darkness in your mind, with a clear light of possibility, your world opens up and so do the opportunities. What is this darkness? Mass media, naysayers, ankle biters, non- believers, and the toxic people not ready to invite change into their lives. It's the inner voice that keeps trying to tell you, you're not good enough or deserving enough. It's the friends and family members that don't share your dreams. It's your own perceived fears, limiting beliefs and past setbacks that prevent you from unleashing the power within.

Work as hard as you can, for as long as you can; and help as many people as you can. To build a legacy business, you have to get yourself out of the way and focus on helping others. The first step is to start. Without action, there's no reaction and nothing will change, if you keep waiting for someday.

Never give up. Even if you just commit 1 hour a day towards building your own dream, it will be worth it 5 to 10 years from now. Working at a 9-5 job may help you create a living, but it won't help you build the life of your dreams. If you can put in 8 hours everyday into building someone else's dream, then why not allocate time towards building your own? Embrace the challenges, setbacks and failures as a forward movement. See the learning from all of your mistakes as special gifts.

Danny creates a ritual of reminding his team members, to get obsessed with their pursuit for success. He asks them, "What are you prepared to do, every single day, to make your dream a reality?" He loves to share a great example of Michael Jordan, one of the all time top basketball players, who trained incessantly to reach new levels. He hated the thought of losing or missing the game-winning shot. He trained for hours, every single day, practicing the basic shots over and over. To change your life, requires a new kind of energy that starts and continues with you taking 100% responsibility for being the maestro of your life. No one else can, or will, do it for you. Danny reflects, "I'm not smarter than the next guy and I know that to reach new levels of success, I have to outwork everyone else."

Similar to Michael Jordan, Danny changed his attitude by creating new success habits. This kind of focus, eventually changes your behaviour, and that's what it's all about! To reach new levels in your life, you have to be willing, to do something new! Each one of Danny's new habits influenced the next, like a domino effect, creating momentum and moving his life forward. "The first thing I needed to do, was release my ego and my pride." He embraced his deeper, driving Why as a new form of inspiration. He believed at a deeper level, supporting his parents would become his driving force and his greater sense of purpose.

One of my favourite books is titled, *The 7 Spiritual Laws of Superheroes*, written by Deepak Chopra and his son, Gotham. The relevance to this chapter is the way in which Deepak brings to light the power of purpose and it's ability to influence all of our actions. It's this commitment to developing and living a more purposeful life that guides superheroes. This powerful energy magnetizes and amplifies their calling in life. When superheroes feel as if they're taken off course they immediately harness the power of their purpose, to instantly pull them back on track. For Danny, his purpose was to make a profound impact on his family. This deeper calling helped him remain bullet proof and resistant to anyone attempting to take him off course.

Another success habit he created was having great posture. It was a new behaviour he had to cultivate. Posture is like an energy force, and it serves as a powerful intention that emits confidence. When people experience your posture, they can feel your confidence in knowing where you're going. Your posture helps create that bulletproof vest, protecting you from whatever outcomes show up in your life. Danny's posture helped him achieve greater levels of success when he began sharing his new opportunity with others. Danny knows his purpose and it drives his actions and his posture every day.

47

~ Dream Bit ~
Big Dreamers Develop Posture

Big Dreamers like, Henry Ford, Thomas Edison, and Steve Jobs, leaned into their purpose and didn't need others to embrace their idea. They were clear as to why they were here and this certainty shaped their posture. Big Dreamers are the modern day superheroes, everyday people that believe, without ego, that they are here to live their one precious life to the fullest.

When you embrace and exist with a defined sense of posture, everything becomes possible. People look at you and take notice of your presence. Some are curious and instantly attracted to it, while others, are inspired to join your cause and be a part of your journey. Not everyone is going to get it, and nor should they, if they all did then the opportunity wouldn't exist! When you embrace a new attitude of serving the many, your purpose takes on new depths of meaning. Your identity instantly shifts from just trying to survive, to the one helping the masses thrive. This was the underlining shift that opened up Danny's world. It didn't happen overnight. In his previous years, he chose a less collaborative approach. He created outcomes of isolation and disconnection. His former attitude, didn't serve the Big Dreamer, living inside of him. When he began focusing on others, his bigger dreams became real and his success accelerated.

Danny began living one of my personal mantras, "a world inspired." Imagine thriving in a world where we all exist to shine a light on others. Imagine the outcomes in our world if 7 billion people helped one another ignite their deeper driving Why. People would wake up to a more purposeful existence and we would create a world of Big Dreamers. By embracing this collective consciousness, of serving one another and helping everyone to live their greatest potential through passion and purpose, we unlock new levels of human possibility. We instantly replace fear, hate, and competition, with deeper levels of love, hope, and gratitude. We would eradicate war and substitute it with resounding global peace. We would eliminate world hunger and economic decline with prosperity. Negativity perpetuated by mass media would no longer exist and thrive in a world filled with love and inspiration. Stealing from others would become a thing of the past, as a result of a world that exists to raise the vibration of the human race. This is the basis for our evolution, as a species. The world is becoming awake to this transformational shift and it's the energy of Big Dreamers that will light the way for all of us.

Through a perilous and arduous journey, Danny uncovered his purpose and ignited his deeper driving Why. He made a conscious choice to take 100% responsibility, for the life he desired to create. He experienced greater levels of fulfillment in serving others. No matter where his journey takes him, he will never dismiss the feelings of being broke, isolated and hungry. He replaced a past sense of hopelessness and despair, with one of inspired possibility. He is no longer alone, lost or disconnected from his family. He lives each day, with greater urgency for his life. He enjoys living a simple life and treasures his time with family and friends. His basic needs are covered and he focuses on helping others get money out of their way, and cultivate deeper connections with what matters most. "I witnessed my dad work everyday from 6:00 a.m. to 8:00 p.m., up until his 82nd year. I now see him falling apart and I want to spend as much time with him as possible." He hardly saw his father as a young boy, and now in his 47th year, Danny is getting to know his dad. When we embrace the power of time as the only true currency, we will make time for what matters, because once it's gone, it's gone.

49

Danny found the way to treasure the moments and make time for what really matters to him. For the first time in his life, he feels a deeper connection to his true self and to his family. He replaced past habits of procrastination with inspired and proactive actions. When he coaches and mentors his team, he inspires a greater sense of urgency within them. He walks along side them, until they have the courage to inspire others to do the same.

~ Dream Bit ~
Big Dreamers Create Time

Big Dreamers don't wait for someday, they know the only way to change their future is to start today. That means embracing a new level of thinking and creating new success habits that drive new behaviours and ultimately shape them into who they are!

They live in the power of today, knowing that it will shape the outcomes of their future.

Here is what I know for certain. You are the creator of your life. You don't get a second chance to try it again. There is no rewind button on the song of your life. You have been given a gift of dreaming bigger and you have the power to imagine a new reality for your life. You have a choice to believe it's possible and you deserve it. You get to choose how you start each day. When you commit to powerful, daily action, your dreams expand. How cool is that! All of us are born as co-creators and it starts with your relentless desire to live as a Big Dreamer now, not someday. Put aside the past, and the current distractions, keeping you from focusing on what matters most.

Danny chose to create a sense of urgency with his life. He made time the most important commodity. He realized his existence is limited, and so, chose to design a life that helped him become closer with his family. "Don't live with the pain of regret, embrace the ones you love now. I know that my time on this earth is limited. Heck, more than half of it is gone and I'm not prepared to go one more day, without living it to the fullest."

He now believes, anything is possible. He inspires this level of confidence in people, helping them arrive at the same realizations he has uncovered. He works hard, but plays harder; and he leads a life, by showing others how to create theirs. He lives with a humble energy and is doing the inner work daily to receive and embrace his success. His dream machine is on full force, as he dreams to help 100 people create a six-figure income and foster deeper a connection with their family.

Like most Big Dreamers, his greatest wish for others is to never stop dreaming. Decide NOW what you want most, and surround yourself with positive people that won't let you stop dreaming. Educate yourself by seeking out opportunities and resources available to you, ones that will help you, take control of your life. Take action by committing to doing something, every single day, to move yourself closer to your goal.

~ Dream Bit ~
Big Dreamers Seek Happiness
Big Dreamers develop the capacity to be happy in any situation. They experience deeper levels of fulfillment by helping others experience joy and inner happiness.

Spending time and creating memories with family and friends is what gives Danny his energy for life. "My greatest wish is to have all of my high school friends be a part of this vision; and to all travel the world together," he shares. We feel as if we have all the time in the world to create our desired lives, and as a result, we have somehow lost the ability to create a greater sense of urgency within ourselves. However, it is only through grasping a deeper awareness of our mortality, that we are forced to prioritize, where and who, we allocate our precious energy. Danny wants to be remembered for having made a difference in the lives of everyone he meets. There's no doubt in my mind, that the energy and vibration in the lives of his friends and family have been taken to new levels; and it is a direct result of this man's purpose to strengthen others. I am honoured to shine a light on this Big Dreamer.

~ A Dedication to Danny from his family ~

Danny's Mom: *My son Danny is hard working, loyal, loving and full of kindness. He always thinks of others.*

Danny's Sister, Susan Gasemy Mitchell: *Danny has always put others first. He has a huge heart and gives 150% all the time. When I look at my children today and talk about Danny, I always say, "Be like your Uncle Danny, dream bigger than you think you can. " We are so very proud of him.*

Danny's sister, Katie Gasemy: *Danny's school reports were all pretty consistent. "Easily distracted in class, constantly daydreaming", one simply wrote, "just wouldn't amount to anything." I stopped reading to find my parents, beaming with pride; and my mom simply saying, "well, they should look at my son now!"*

Danny's Father, Gasem Gasemy: *Throughout primary and secondary school, he needed help. Some years, he was tutored. He was very upset with the situation and said, "Daddy, do not waste your money. I already know all of those things they are trying to teach me." Danny had special abilities, to repair and fix instruments and machines. One day, my oldest son said to me, "Daddy be kind with Danny he has somehow fixed a broken motorcycle and he is very proud of his accomplishment, even though, he didn't ride or have a motorcycle of his own. Danny was very kind to animals. He had about half a dozen snakes, running from 2 to 6 feet in length. One day, one of his snakes escaped from the cage and everyone was waiting for Danny to find it. Danny found it in the garden room and carefully placed it back in the cage, putting us all at ease. Along with all his other amazing attributes, Danny is also very kind and affectionate towards others. With all the obstacles he faced, he still achieved his goal as a successful entrepreneur. We are so proud of all of his achievements. We love you son.*

2. Gerry Visca

WHY do you want it?

"Decide what you want most, take action and go get it!" Gerry Visca

I *exist* to creatively inspire people and their ideas to action. I'm compelled to share with you my journey, from building buildings to building up people. Every challenge I have faced has brought me a step forward. Every crossroad has unfolded a new chapter in my life and ultimately ignited the only question that matters, why am I here?

I was raised in Chippewa, 30 minutes outside of Niagara Falls, Canada. To know my life, you need to open a window into my mother's journey. My mother was only 14 when her parents arranged for her to marry my father in Italy. Growing up I wasn't aware of her perilous journey and the nightmare it was to travel from her home in Italy to Canada. Her story could be a book or a movie. To say her marriage was emotionally and physically abusive is an understatement! My parents didn't have much of anything when they first started out. My father was a carpenter and he travelled back and forth from Italy to France, with my mother, trying to get whatever odd jobs he could before eventually making their way to Canada.

Everyday was a struggle for my mom to survive. A few years ago, she shared with me that she had a great desire to take her life, when she was 7 months pregnant with me. Many days and nights, she was completely alone, hungry, and isolated. With the pressure of raising my two brothers in what was an abusive and poor environment, she lost the will to survive and took an overdose of sleeping pills. A day later, she was found not breathing. The doctors termed my birth as nothing short of miraculous. It's one of the reasons why she refers to me as her "little miracle."

Growing up in Chippewa, we didn't have much; stockings at Christmas time consisted of my father's socks filled with walnuts and tangerines, yet I always felt my mother's love. The greatest challenge in my early years was witnessing the physical abuse inflicted upon my mother and my brothers. The day I was knocked out unconscious is one that still haunts me. I vividly recall helping my father build a garden shed, I had said something that upset him, so I ran as fast as I could to get away from him, only to be knocked out by the hammer he propelled at my back.

My mother eventually summoned up the courage to divorce him. There came a point where she had enough and was prepared to stand on her own, and surround my brothers and I with unconditional love. We moved to Niagara Falls and lived in a small two-bedroom apartment. The space was tight and we had to share bedrooms, but what outweighed those challenges was the love and creativity my mom nurtured in us.

~ Dream Bit ~
Big Dreamers Take Action

Big Dreamers don't wait for someday to appear. They take action with a greater sense of urgency for their lives. They don't wait for things or others to change. They become the change they are seeking. Big Dreamers act on inspired thoughts.

The creativity of drawing always helped me live in the moment. I would lose myself for hours in these illustrations. Around the age of 6, my mom even signed me up for professional art lessons at a local studio. She instilled within me a series of profound insights, one of them being the art of visualization. She taught me how to close my eyes and see the end results of what I was creating clearly in my mind. Every piece of art I illustrated always started with the end picture in my mind.

My mom was a talented seamstress and wedding dress designer. I often watched her live the art of visualization. I remember one day, gazing at her with curiosity as she sketched out a wedding dress. I asked her why she closed her eyes. She lovingly responded, "I'm seeing the end result of what I want this dress to look like in my mind, closing my eyes helps me create it."

Over the years, I learned to master this one skill she taught me, especially in competitive sports. Around the age of 10, I followed my middle brother, Salvatore, into the world of tennis. I trained every day, from morning till dusk with friends at the public courts. I never missed watching a *Wimbledon* tennis tournament and visualized playing tennis like my idols: Ivan Lendl, Bjorn Borg and Jimmy Connors. After years of training, I went on to challenge my brother in a major tournament, and then onto becoming ranked as one of South Western Ontario's top tennis juniors. Throughout high school, tennis was always at the forefront. It instilled confidence and a sense of purpose in me.

~ Dream Bit ~

Big Dreamers Visualize

Big Dreamers master the art of visualization by fixating on the outcome of what they desire to create. They see and feel the emotion of actually being there, in the moment. They intentionally implant positive thoughts into their sub conscious, influencing their choices and behaviours.

My mother was passionate about empowering women. She opened up her own sewing and teaching centre called, *Lucy's Sewing Centre.* Her students praised her teachings and her reputation expanded. Her manager eventually introduced her to her older brother, a special man, named Norman, whom she later married. I was around 13 at the time and like most teenage boys, I wasn't the easiest to get along with. I wasn't fond of rules and challenged the status quo, every chance I had. My mom had different plans for us. She decided we would relocate to Mississauga from our small hometown, of Niagara Falls. I eventually came around, since most of the major tennis tournaments, were hosted in the Toronto area. Changing high school was one of the most challenging events as a young teen. The academic part of high school was a challenge for me. Not that I wasn't intelligent, I was simply distracted with tennis and socializing. I had a knack for talking to people and making them feel good. This was the seed of the "creative coach" inside of me. I'm sure if I applied myself to my academic studies, I would have done much better than just getting by. My morning routine consisted of waking up at 5:00am, catching 3 busses to the tennis club to practice. After school, I headed back for another 3 hours of tennis camp. It was my life force and all I wanted to do was get better, so I could eventually travel to the US on a tennis scholarship. Unfortunately, I always ignored the importance of stretching and warming up before my matches. Years of poor conditioning and an unorthodox twist serve, eventually led to a fracture in my lower vertebrae. Any chance of a tennis scholarship was over.

I was angry, sad, depressed and felt as if my identity as a ranked tennis junior was gone. I can see clearly now, I was defined by my status as a competitive athlete. When it was gone, I didn't know who I was anymore. I even became angry with my parents and lashed out at their lack of support towards my tennis career. Around the age of 16, my parents were at their wits end with me, they had enough. They gave me an ultimatum, either enrol in college or enlist in the army. So, I chose to study architecture in Toronto that next year. Living in Toronto and studying architecture was a whole new awakening for me. I loved the energy and finally came to grips with letting tennis go and closing off that chapter in my life. I was enthralled with becoming an inspiring architect.

I always preferred to draw historical and classical buildings, like the Coliseum, in Rome or the Parthenon, in Ancient Greece. My curiosity for the architectural world, expanded and I craved a deeper understanding of the psychology and behaviour of why and how people interacted in spaces. Architecture seemed to bridge my interests and my passions.

~ Dream Bit ~

Big Dreamers Do What They Love

As I'm writing this chapter, ironically, I'm reading a book called: F**k it, do what you love! Big Dreamers find the joy in doing what they love. They don't allocate energy towards things that don't fill them up with tremendous joy.

As a young boy, my teachers often placed me in the corner of a room. I was the embarrassing example to the other kids. They labelled me a "day dreamer" and every report card indicated a whack of concerns, with my incessant need to socialize with others. What can I say? I love to talk! What my teachers failed to observe was my passion for dreaming, creating and connecting. I was inspired to contribute to the well being of others kids, and I knew I could always make them laugh with my presence and my energy. Oh, if my teachers could see me now, on stage connecting with my audiences!

~ Dream Bit ~

Big Dreamers Become Curious

A deep sense of wonder and awe for the world exists within the minds of Big Dreamers. It's ignited at an early age and they become fascinated with the world around them. They question everything and continually wonder why.

Around the age of 18, I decided to move out on my own. I had already experienced a taste of living in Toronto, while attending college, so I was ready to forge ahead and create my independence. I moved out into a brand new condo, with my best friend and for the first time, I truly felt as if I was creating my life. Upon graduating in 1997 with honours, I was offered an intern position with a prestigious, architectural firm; however, I chose a more diverse role with the City of Toronto. Most of my classmates, were taking roles in traditional firms, but I wanted to do something different; I wanted to stand out.

~ Dream Bit ~
Big Dreamers ZIG When Others ZAG!

Big Dreamers don't follow the pack and create their own way. They see differentiation, as a virtue. They break away from traditional models and challenge the status quo.

I met my former wife around the age of 19. I was enthralled with this new and committed relationship. Up to this point, I only experienced casual relationships and was reluctant to open up my heart to anyone. We got engaged within the first 18 months of dating and married young. I didn't know what the hell I was doing! Her parents were totally against us getting married before she graduated, so we decided to wait. She was inspired by my independence and she too craved breaking away from her conservative parents.

~ Dream Bit ~
Big Dreamers Crave Independence

Big Dreamers are highly independent. It starts at a very young age and influences their career choices later on in life. They prefer to blaze their own trail. Big Dreamers stand out from the crowd and often struggle with attempting to fit in.

After several years of promotions, while working for The City of Toronto, I decided it was time to enter the private sector and I pursued a senior position in a private architectural firm. They had two offices one in Toronto and one in London. The London office had recently landed one of the largest healthcare restructuring projects in Canada, and they needed a project manager to head up operations.

My wife and I had been married for four years now with a young daughter. I loved her, yet I struggled at managing the multiple priorities in my life. Following college, I had chosen to pursue a second architectural degree while working full time. In retrospect, not a great idea at the start of a marriage! Just before moving to London, I was undertaking my final thesis, working as an architect for the City of Toronto and now, relocating my family to a new city.

Life in London was challenging. Helping establish the London firm was a monumental task. There were no procedures in place and I was surrounded by daily chaos. I found myself working 11-hour days and having to work on my thesis project in the evenings and on weekends. Within 24 months, I graduated with an honours degree in Architecture and help expand the London firm from 5 to 75 people. The time away from my family took its toll on all of us. My wife felt alone and disconnected and I didn't know how to be present. I knew something had to change.

~ Dream Bit ~

Big Dreamers Channel Change

Big Dreamers see change as a gift from the universe, helping them get into alignment with their life purpose. Instead of resisting change, they learn to become the change they wish to experience in the world.

I chose to resign from the firm, and set up my own hybrid agency in London. I had a passion for marketing and presentation, so it made sense to combine these creative talents I had nurtured over the years. This was the first time I felt as if I owned my own time. My wife was initially pleased with the idea. It seemed to connect us in new ways and we always dreamed of creating something of our own. The next 24 months, I poured myself into setting up my own creative agency. I didn't know what the hell I was doing, but I knew why. I wanted to help my clients stand out through compelling communications. I was quickly branded as the "presentation master", helping a myriad of clients win in highly competitive situations. I had a talent for extracting their essence and presenting clients in a more compelling and meaningful way than their competitors. I ended up expanding the firm from 2 employees to 11 in the first 3 years. We expanded our offices and my overhead quickly multiplied. I can see clearly now the move to London was a step towards creating my own way and my own agency.

Big Dreamers

Big Dreamers Ignite Their Unique Abilities

Big Dreamers follow their unique abilities. They find joy in applying their innate talents through service to others. They become aware of their special gifts and look for opportunities to live them. Their unique ability feeds their purpose and helps them experience more meaningful outcomes in their lives.

Meanwhile, my wife and I decided to have another child. Our oldest daughter, Emma was almost 5 and we didn't want her to grow up alone. Our second daughter, Sophie, entered our lives and I felt a huge surge of love and gratitude flowing through me. My wife decided to join my agency and support our growth. I was drowning in keeping up with the many roles, Creative Director, Business Developer and CEO. I felt a huge sense of pressure every month to bring in projects just to keep the doors open! My monthly overhead was reaching up to $70K. I attempted to bring on sales people to offset this pressure, but quickly found myself spending even more time overseeing their efforts. I didn't see a clear way out. I once again found myself at a crossroads something had to change.

~ Dream Bit ~

Big Dreamers Listen To Their Intuition

Big Dreamers are guided by their intuition. They sense the world around them and recognize when it's time for a change. They shield themselves from external influences and step into action with a sense of ease and flow knowing every action opens new doors.

Eventually, the pressures of owning our own business seemed to add to our stress and affected our home life. We found ourselves separating for weeks on end. Seven years into our marriage, she was ready to leave London with the kids and move back closer to her family. I'll never forget the feeling of standing inside our empty London living room watching the movers remove the few remaining boxes. A part of me was seeking independence, yet flashes of my family leaving haunted me. After a restless night, I woke up at 5:00am and drove out to my family, where my wife was staying temporarily, and poured out my heart to her. I wasn't prepared to end this 7-year marriage, so I collapsed the lease on my rental loft and moved back in with my family.

~ Dream Bit ~
Big Dreamers Feel Their Life

Big Dreamers are connected to a deeper sense of being. They look at every event in their lives, as a connector to something more profound. They act through a greater sense of love, for they recognize it will lead to a more compelling way.

My wife and I started a new journey. We opened up a second office in Hamilton and I decided to collapse the original London location and restructure our team. I had a long-held desire to simplify operations and reduce my commuting time between offices. I focused our business development on larger branding-type projects and chose to nurture longer-term clients. As a Creative Director, I mastered the art of extracting a company's deeper reason for being. I can see clearly now, this was building the foundation for my future passion, as the *#WhyGuy*. Although this streamlining created greater balance in my agency, a new challenges soon surfaced. We were now experiencing 6-month wait times for payments from our larger clients, and a series of unpaid accounts created a financial strain on our line of credit. I knew something had to change and that's when I began to write and later published my first two books: *What Have You Got To Win®* and *Kick Starters®*. These books summarized my passion for creating a new passive income stream, while sharing my growing insights in the area of presentation and communication.

I'll never forget the day that changed everything! It was a Thursday and I was driving to a networking meeting. I remember a surge of energy coursing through my veins. I pulled over to the side of the road and as I closed my eyes I noticed my breath and experienced visions of inspiring thousands of people. I was no longer fulfilled with the type of work I was directing. I wasn't interested in managing complex clients or a large staff. I was tired of chasing unpaid accounts and having to manage a growing overhead. Once again, I knew something had to change, and fast, or we would eventually maximize our line of credit. My deeper reason for serving others was becoming increasingly clear. *"I exist to inspire people and their ideas to action"*, became my new mantra. I dreamed of writing and publishing books, touring the world, and inspiring everyday people to create their desired lives. The Big Dreamer within me was cranked way up and I had visions of a coaching centre that would ignite entrepreneurs to uncover their passion and purpose. I couldn't wait to share this new revelation with my partner and my team. Little did I know, my dream and life mission, I was craving to create would not be received very well. They resisted any kind of change that would impact their lives.

Leading up to this revelation, my wife had recognized I was in a state of metamorphosis and she gifted me a set of audio discs titled, *The Success Principles®*, by author Jack Canfield. Over the next 12 months, I immersed myself into these discs, absorbing every word Jack shared. Words like, "take 100% responsibility for the life you desire to create" and "know why you are here", filled my heart and soul. I was on fire and ready to forge ahead with a new life mission. I felt like the great Italian sculptor and painter, Michelangelo. I could envision the statue inside the block of marble; I just needed to carve it out by discarding the pieces of my life that didn't serve me.

My wife and I had managed to slowly move our lives forward, yet she sensed I was unfulfilled. It was a Saturday and we had been arguing for the past couple of days, so she hadn't spoken to me. She just looked at me and said, "Gerry, I want a divorce. I want you to be happy and find your path that will bring you more fulfillment." At first, I was blown away and in tears. I hated the idea of a divorce and humbly asked her to reconsider. After a couple of hours of feeling what she was sharing with me, I sensed she was right and I made an instant choice to feel only love and gratitude for the life and beautiful daughters we created together. I too wanted her to find the love she deserved.

~ Dream Bit ~

Big Dreamers Lead With Love

Big Dreamers choose to lead through the power of love. They let this energy guide all of their actions. They push away the temporary fear of being isolated and alone. They embrace an open heart and fill themselves up with higher levels of love and gratitude.

I chose to restructure our agency, yet again, and moved into a new collaborative office space that just opened in Burlington, Ontario. I loved the openness and energy of this space and believed it would lend itself to my new vision of a coaching centre. In just a few months of settling in *Ignite Idea Centre®* was alive! I moved into my studio loft, we had been operating out of for the past 5 years. Our separation moved along fairly smoothly with my wife maintaining her role as a partner in the agency. My daughters loved spending time with me in the loft and we travelled together cultivating a new connection. I chose to invest in myself through personal development. I published my 3rd book called, *Get Creative®*, which cultivated my Why - to inspire others to create their desired lives. And so, the reinvention of my branding agency into an inspirational coaching centre was underway.

~ Dream Bit ~

Big Dreamers Love Change

Big Dreamers recognize that for things to change, they have to drive the change. They embrace temporary discomfort by fixating on the end prize of what they are creating. Through gratitude they are able to open their hearts in order to allow the love to rush in.

I didn't know what the hell I was doing when I created this centre, but I always knew why and that was to inspire everyday people to create their desired lives!

In 2007 I created a *Branding Boot Camp®* tour, that eventually went on to inspire thousands of people across Canada and it even attracted one of the most prestigious speaking bureaus, the National Speakers Bureau, to represent me on the world stage. I had an intention of speaking internationally and even printed new business cards with the title, Author and International Speaker. Soon after, I attracted speaking assignments as far as Istanbul. I was now regarded as the "branding guru". I was quickly forging ahead by replacing marketing-type projects with consulting, coaching, events and speaking opportunities. I felt as if my dream was unfolding.

~ Dream Bit ~
Big Dreamers Are Intentional

Big Dreamers harness the energy of the moment by deciding on what they want most and share their intention with the world. They choose to live their lives with positivity and reject the naysayers. They believe in their vision and carve out the time to live it each day.

My inspirational vision was expanding the more I stepped into this way of being. I forged a new mastermind group and attracted collaborative partners. I attracted a series of media interviews, radio, print, and television. I was featured on the hit show, *CBC Fortune Hunters*, as they profiled one of my clients. I was continually in a state of innovation, creating *Big Think Events* and evenings of inspired thinking. I was attracting coaching clients and touring my new book, *Get Creative*. I had a long-held desire of sharing stage with my mentor, Jack Canfield. I fixated on this vision for over 6 months. Then one day, I received a call from an event planner inquiring if I would consider speaking with Jack and other speakers from the new hit book and movie *The Secret*. When I met Jack, I shared my vision of inspiring 1 million people to action and the impact his book had on me igniting my reinvention.

The greatest challenge during my reinvention, was attempting to attract revenue, while carving out the time to focus on my inspirational work. This is one of the greatest challenges Big Dreamers face at the start of their reinvention, they don't commit to carving out the time and they resist the necessary changes that show up. What I know now is that when you commit to living your dream life, at first it seems as if your life is falling apart, but the more you step into the change the more your vision starts to unfold. I can see clearly now that to live my bigger dream of inspiring 1 million people, as an author and speaker, things in my life had to change and I had to allocate the time to make them change.

I still had to face the challenges of everyday life, and unfortunately, our agency was now close to maximizing our line of credit. All I wanted to do was charge ahead with my new inspirational work, but this looming debt seemed to pin me down. The year of 2008 rolled in and with it the economic meltdown, which was occurring in the United States made its way to Canada. The banking institutions were in major lockdown mode and began calling in all of the outstanding loans from businesses. I received a call from my bank, demanding our full $200K line of credit to be paid off in 30 days. I shared the news with my partner and reassured her we could get through this, if we put an immediate plan into place. I sat there alone in my red chair, contemplating the events that transpired over the past 14 months. I built a new level of connection with my daughters, managed to streamline my business, ignited the start of my bigger dreams as a speaker and author, and attracted a new loving relationship into my life. I fixated on dedicating 100% of my attention towards living a life of inspiration. I removed many of the barriers that prevented me from carving out this new life. The only thing I hadn't removed was the legacy of financial loan accumulated with the growth of my agency. I was at risk of losing my new home and I wasn't taking a salary for several months, as part of my recovery plan. I managed to restructure a financing arrangement allowing me to pay off the total loan over the next 5 years. The only caveat was I had to come up with $75K in 30 days. I managed to land a couple of branding projects and even reached out to my brothers for a temporary loan in order to satisfy the bank's requirements. This was by far one of the greatest challenges in my life, but I knew I had to move through this challenge in order to create my desired life. I believed in myself and in my abilities to push through the temporary pain.

Despite our recovery plan, my partner had a difficult time dealing with all this; she was in fear mode and chose to leave the agency, and me, with the responsibility of paying off the total loan and carrying all the risk. I felt alone and abandoned. I did everything I could over the next several months to keep my agency alive. I managed to attract a global branding contract with a German medical device company that needed someone creative to help establish a strong brand presence in Canada. I was thrilled and negotiated a monthly retainer that would allow me to pay back my brothers in 12 months, while still supporting my financial commitments to my daughters.

The transitional period during 2009-2010 represented one of the greatest personal growth periods in my life. I hunkered down, simplified my lifestyle and managed to pay off over 65% of the bank loan and even pay back my brothers. I chose to carve out one day a week to writing and publishing my 4th book, *The Innovation Gap®* with an intention of bridging inspiration and innovation, as I had witnessed a gap in organizations which impacted their ability to collaborate, create and communicate more effectively among teams. I built a strong connection with the head office in Germany and upon completing my 12-month contract I managed to win a series of new global opportunities in Berlin. I chose to maintain a positive relationship with my former wife and business partner, because in any given moment we can always choose how we wish to respond. That's the magic bullet making better choices that continually move our lives, and our relationships in an upward direction. When do these choices show up? Well, in every moment of your life.

~ Dream Bit ~
Big Dreamers Get The Work Done

Big Dreamers don't waste time faltering or blaming others. They focus only on the task at hand. They don't rely on hoping and wishing as a means to manifest their dreams. They create plans, set powerful and measurable goals, and take action on high pay off activities.

During these 12-14 months of reinvention, I also developed new success habits like, meditating every morning, losing weight and developing a healthier lifestyle. I replaced TV watching with listening to inspiring audio programs and enhanced my personal development skills. I surrounded myself with vision boards and read my affirmations, out loud, every day. I created a gratitude journal and every night I filled it with encouraging words for the life I was creating. In my mind, I chose to fixate on the feeling of seeing the bank loan completely paid in full. I envisioned a life of inspiration and poured myself into serving others.

In only a few short years, I managed to completely pay off the bank loan and swore to never take another one again! It was now 2011, my creative coaching business was thriving, my inspirational and publishing work expanded and I launched the *Defyeneurs*® movement. I was fulfilling a long-held desire to create a movement and a platform that shines a light on everyday people doing extraordinary things. I attracted the love of my life, Angela, who I have been existing with for the past 5 years. We met at a coaching centre in Burlington, Ontario and it was love at first sight. The moment I saw her, standing there, I was instantly pulled into her energy. She has witnessed the realization of my bigger dream to inspire 1 Million Why's and I am so grateful for her.

After meeting Angela, I reconnected with Jack Canfield and shared my reinvention, and my intention to serve the world with my purpose. He contributed the foreword to two of the *Defyeneurs*® book series and recently published my story in his latest book, *Living the Success Principles*®. Angela and I continue to travel the world, inspiring, creating and igniting the deeper Why in everyone we meet. My 13th book titled, *I Don't Know What The HELL I'm Doing®*, published last year, captures my top 9 insights for helping readers answer the only question that matters, "Why am I here?"

~ Dream Bit ~
Big Dreamers Are Persistent

Big Dreamers are persistent in creating their desired life. Big Dreamers reject the naysayers. They see the end result of their desires clearly in their minds and they are relentless in their pursuit to see the end result realized.

The *Defyeneurs®* movement is now rapidly reaching 1 million impressions. We have published over 10 issues of our inspired magazine publication and 5 collaborative books with over 100 authors. I enjoy living a debt-free life filled with daily inspiration. My life partner, Angela, and I enjoy the simple things in life. We travel the world inspiring, publishing and shining our love and light on others. The events that occurred over the past 7-9 years became the catalyst for the greatest reinvention of my life. Sometimes the first idea is the first step towards making your dream a reality. Not every one of my ideas stood on it's own. Some of them were more profitable than others, but the true magic of the idea was kick starting the dream. Here's a look at how some of these ideas influenced my bigger dreams:

- **My first book and audio CD titled:** *What Have You Got To Win?*® ignited the next 14 books of my publishing career and I learned to carve out the time for writing.

- **My 3rd book project titled:** *Kick Starters*® attracted media interviews and ignited my 5th book, *THINQ*, which includes 3 sets of *THINQ* decks (51 inspiring questions) per deck that we use at events.

- *Ignite Idea Centre*® ignited my coaching practice and my formal *Ignite Coaching Program*, which has served hundreds of inspired entrepreneurs.

- **My 4th book titled,** *The Innovation Gap*® attracted Angela, the love of my life. This energy connected me to Think Spot in Burlington, where I coached dozens of entrepreneurs.

- *Big Think & Branding Boot Camps*® ignited my global speaking career and connected me to world-class speakers and a Canadian tour that inspired several thousand kids.

- **The TV Pilot** ignited the *Defyeneurs*® movement, a global magazine and book series, and publishing the Big Dreamers in this book.

- **My 14th Book titled,** *Big Dreamers* has already ignited my 15th book, *Women Who Influence*, which will launch in 2017.

This is the power in taking action on an idea. It opens the way for bigger and better ideas, which eventually, ignites your dream.

As I sit here writing my chapter in this epic book, I glance over to my 16-year-old daughter lying in a hospital bed, fighting stage 3 cancer. She has been such an inspiration to me, since the day she was born. She connected our family, as a beautiful light, during the darkest times. She faces her greatest life challenge with grace, dignity and tremendous courage. She reminds me of the value of time and to never wait a moment longer, to embrace everything life has to offer. Witnessing her battle with cancer has ignited an ever-deeper calling in my life and challenged me to live my legacy now!

My wish for you, my dear reader, is to decide what you want most, take action, fail forward, and don't stop pursuing what you desire most in life! If you are not on fire about your work and your relationships, then end it now; life is just too damn short for anything else! You deserve to live and love your life to the fullest. You were born as a being of light with unbridled possibility. Somewhere in your life, you may have been told to take off your "super cape" and stay grounded with the rest of the world. I say the hell with listening to the ankle biters, throw that cape back on, look up, aim high, and fly! This book is your calling to turn on your dream machine and ignite your deeper driving Why. The world needs Big Dreamers now, more than ever. When you choose to ignite your deeper driving Why, then we all benefit, for the World is Helped by You.

Scan this code to check out the energy of my philosophy,
I Don't Know What The Hell I'm Doing!

LIFE ISN'T ABOUT ASKING HOW. LIFE IS ABOUT KNOWING WHY

~ Gerry Visca

3. Aana Camp

Who do you want to be?

"When we open our hearts and minds to others, we open new doors and avenues to our own success; finding possibilities that may not have been revealed had we been alone." ~ Aana Camp

Aana Camp *exists* to help others create a stronger belief in themselves. She is one of five kids who grew up in a wonderful household, in the Los Angeles area. Her mother always instilled in her a high level of belief. She grew up knowing she could be and have anything she set her mind to. Her mother encouraged her to visualize daily, and had her imagine the things she desired most in life; knowing if she focused on them they would come true. At a very early age, she believed if she could see and feel it in her mind, she would make it a reality.

Reflecting back, she shares an overwhelming sense of gratitude, for what her mom instilled in her at such an early age. "This inspired process of visualization impacted all areas of my life," she explains. She cultivated an ability to see clearly in her mind what she desired most to create. Her younger years were greatly influenced by her dynamic mother, who was always experiencing new and exciting things in the world.

Aana had a wonderful upbringing and a great family life, yet there was something that she was searching for that she couldn't quite define. "Unlike others around me, who had a sense of what they wanted to do with their lives, I was unsettled with the direction I would take," she noted. She had a desire to remain open and optimistic with her education and future career. Many of her friends that headed into college and seemed to know what direction their future would be. "It was as if they had no other choice after they graduated and moved into their pre-selected careers," she shares. Aana didn't follow the same path, but what she knew for certain and at an early age was she had no desire to work for someone else or play by someone else's rules.

This earlier mindset influenced varying types of careers, including selling real estate, which she developed quite a passion for. She was ecstatic about finding people their dream homes and possessed a keen sense of style and decor. She found herself existing in this field, for 10 years, while still being open to new opportunities. At one point, she considered getting into the dental field or even becoming a veterinarian, but neither felt quite right. "I hadn't tapped into the direction that would ultimately fulfill me," she shares. There was one thing in life that she always had a long-held desire for and that was to get married and start a family.

After getting married, she chose to maintain her real estate career, primarily for the flexibility to travel with her entrepreneurial husband. In her late 20's, she gave birth to a beautiful son named, Skylar. Her flexible lifestyle permitted her to stay home with Skylar, for the first 5 years of his life. "Staying at home and raising my son, was something that meant the world to me." She always dreamed and relished at the idea of being a part of her child's life during those tender years. And working as a real-estate agent enabled her to work from home, which was wonderful. However, the increasing decline in the economy had a major impact on her business. She saw the incoming recession as a gift and a sign, to leave the real estate industry and spend more time with her son.

These were challenging times for Aana and her marriage though. She found the relationship and connection with her husband deteriorating. She experienced a great sense of uneasiness for her future. What she knew for certain, at this stage of her three year old son's life was she wanted to surround him with love and positivity. She knew that it was time for a change and the inevitable outcome would lead to a divorce.

Even though she remained optimistic, a wave of uncertainty washed over her. Five years transpired, since she stepped away from a real estate career, so there was no desire to re-enter and rebuild her clientele within that industry. "These emotional times, had me questioning, how I was going to reinvent myself and provide for my son. Up to this point, I felt I hadn't invented myself yet," she recounts. She was driven to define the bigger meaning of her life and she wanted to create something lucrative for her and her son. Something with purpose and meaning.

She spent long nights asking and reflecting on big questions. She was determined to chart a path of independence. All of these events, crack opened her universe and the thrill of existing as an entrepreneur rushed in! Eventually, the housing market began showing signs of resuscitation. Aana responded by creating an innovative niche in that industry through the supply of game room furnishings. She keenly observed how people didn't know how to finish a dining room area within a newly purchased home. A spark of innovation inspired her to furnish the large and empty spaces for homeowners. "I created an intention of becoming the go to supplier for high-end game room furnishings in the residential market," she recounted. Shortly after, she attracted an expert who built and sold pool tables for private parties. Upon researching the landscape of pool table construction, she felt she could provide homeowners with a product of far greater value. "It was at this point, when my little pool table business took flight," she recounts.

~ Dream Bit ~
Big Dreamers Invent Themselves

Big Dreamers channel discomfort into creativity and momentum. They create incredible momentum in moving their lives forward. They take 100% responsibility for attracting the people and resources to advance their big dreams.

She created her business by seeing and being open to creative opportunities. She took action and through the *Penny Saver* was able to effectively create a significant demand for her new niche business. At the start of her business, she quickly demonstrated higher value to residential households. With a strong sense of determination and persistence she grew her business little by little.

People from the surrounding area loved her ads in the *Penny Saver* and booked private appointments to visit her bustling showroom. She quickly ascertained that her business growth was limited to the amount of zip codes within a 2-hour radius from her showroom. "I knew I had to extend my reach," she said. She tested her expanded business model in Las Vegas, by using a local phone number she forwarded to her cell phone. By writing her ads in the Las Vegas *Penny Saver*, together with a local phone number, she began creating a larger demand for her pool table business. She eventually created a satellite showroom space in Las Vegas, close to the airport, to respond to the increased waiting list of phone numbers she collected. She strategically organized and coordinated these new Las Vegas showings in one day. This enabled her to drop her son off at grade school, fly to Vegas, see her growing list of clients and fly back to be there at the end of the day to pick him up. "I was doing it all. I answered the incoming calls from two locations, set up two showrooms and facilitated the private appointments with prospective customers," she recounted. This model was so successful that she duplicated it across Denver, Dallas, Las Vegas and Scottsdale.

With the Internet quickly becoming the way of the future, it allowed her business model to grow exponentially. In the earlier days she had attempted to move to the internet, but it proved challenging for her as this was not yet an established or proven medium. Unlike today, consumers were uncomfortable spending thousand of dollars online. With this no longer being the case, she expanded her empire and created an infrastructure to support the challenging transportation logistics of shipping and assembling pool tables across the country. Upon the set up of this massive undertaking, she managed to attract one of the largest retailers to support her expanding enterprise. Aana was quickly becoming one of the largest suppliers of game room furniture and supplies across the country, and eventually became the sole supplier of *Costco's* e-commerce site.

After pouring years of energy towards the innovation, set up and creation of this company, she attracted a buyer and ended up selling her business, in 2005, with the hope she could retire. Following the sale of her company, she purchased her dream home and was living there with her son. It was a majestic property overlooking the ocean. It represented a significant milestone and brought to life a long-held desire for an ocean front property. The future for Aana and her son looked bright, or so she thought.

To her astonishment, one year after the purchase, the company declared bankruptcy and defaulted on the payments she was entitled to for the next 10 years. Everything she had worked for had now crumbled in front of her eyes. Her business and her future income connected to it evaporated. This major turn of events put her into a very compromising situation. "I had to choose whether to keep my dream home, I worked tirelessly for, or downsize." It had been her hope that with the sale of her company she could finally stay home and care for her son, a long-held desire that was now fading away. "What meant more to me than anything was providing my son with the memory of a stay-at-home mom," she noted. She didn't want her son to remember her as a workaholic. Sadly, the payments that were supposed to last for 10 years ran out just before the second year, and she was now forced to re-examine her life and chart a whole new course.

~ Dream Bit ~

Big Dreamers See Every Challenge As An Opportunity For Growth

Big Dreamers re-evaluate their current circumstances by fixating on the end prize of what they desire to create most. They harness the power of the moment and release the energy of the past. Each failure leads them closer and closer to their goal. Let go of judgment and the energy of the past, it doesn't serve your bigger purpose in the moment!

Aana faced significant challenges with grace, courage and creativity. She made a conscious decision to reinvent herself. She was not prepared to give up on her son, or her dreams of creating freedom and financial independence. So, she approached every challenge as an opportunity to discover her untapped potential.

She was introduced to the world of network marketing and was blown away by this type of business model. She had experienced a business that owned 100% of her time and overhead costing her over $70k monthly to run the company. "I was intrigued by the idea of owning 1% of thousands of other people's time and energy," she recalls. "I wondered if this could be a viable model worth exploring." She quickly noticed people earning unlimited sums of money, with a small upfront investment, and virtually no monthly overhead. She loved the idea of creating a new form of income that didn't depend solely on her efforts. She was ready to trade the past energy of selling her time for money for a residual-type income. She could see clearly now, and her dream machine was cranked up full throttle! She tested two different companies and experienced very little success, even after three years of focus and energy. She was still optimistic that this model may be the answer to her long-held desires and dreams of independence though.

She needed a life raft and she needed it fast. She was carrying over $40,000 in credit card debt and was faced with the fear of losing her dream home and the lifestyle she worked so hard to create. Aana shared with me the pride she experienced, as an adult woman, in creating her own way. The independence meant the world to her, and it continued to drive her vision forward. She knew her funds would eventually run out though and she had to make a change, quickly.

Soon after, a colleague approached her and shared an opportunity to join a new anti-aging company that just opened its doors. "I had no idea that trying this little bottle of night cream would transform my entire life," she shares. "I had been praying for months, that an opportunity would reveal itself, and low and behold, it appeared in a 4 inch bottle of night cream," she adds.

An emotional Aana shares with me how she used to stand out on her deck, peering out to the ocean and up at the sky, with her arms spread wide, praying to God for a sign. She would say, "God, I know you've created me for something so much bigger." She believed in herself and she knew in her heart that God had a bigger plan for her. She would also pray, "God you know me, you created me, what is it that you want me to do - put it in my path and make it obvious." Swelling up with tears she later noted, "I knew I was put on this earth to do more than just make a living."

Her earlier years represented, what she defines as her learning years. When I asked her to reflect on the obstacles that got in the way of dreaming big, she laughingly shared that it was either boredom or lack of patience! She was always a stellar student, who excelled in her courses. She would effortlessly achieve a 4.0 GPA in high school, the signs of a genius in the making. She had an innate gift of seeing beyond an immediate opportunity to the end result. She recalls how her dad would often say, she didn't need to go to college and waste four years of her life. She developed the mentality at an early age that she didn't need college, which pleased her dad, since her family didn't have the means to pay for five college tuitions. Looking back now and despite her incredible and entrepreneurial achievements, she does regret not attending college, simply for the experience of it.

In her earlier years, she believed anything was possible. She was a crusader and driven to be her own boss. She was an independent and proud woman that wanted to blaze her own path. This instinct drove her to become the beautiful, proud and independent woman she is today.

The "pool table empire" of her life, is what she calls her "earning journey". "I now define this part of my current life, as my "serving journey"," she adds. She can see clearly now, that her struggle and discomfort led her to exactly where she needed to be. She knew in her heart she was meant to serve the many and make a difference in other peoples lives.

Big Dreamers Are Driven By A Bigger Purpose

Big Dreamers have an inner knowing and they bring this feeling to the forefront and they ignite it with greater intention. They connect the dots and the learning's from their past, through the art of synchronicity.

Big Dreamers remain open to the energy of the universe and act on inspired thoughts.

Her greater intention was fuelled by her purpose to make a difference in the lives of 100 women. She prayed for more than a financial windfall, but rather, a way to inspire others to create their own financial independence. It was this inner belief in herself that lit the flame and ignited her greatest re-invention. Through faith, grace and intentionality, she knew she could move mountains. Her laser-focused intention made her confident that something big was on the horizon, and she was ready to receive it and pay it forward. She didn't need to know the whole path she just believed her resolve and faith would ignite the way.

Aana learned how to intensify her focus and desire for what she wanted to create in her life. She was able to put aside her fears and fixate on the end prize - a life filled with greater purpose. She shares with me how this success habit, of remaining fully open to the gifts from above, would always serve her greater good. It was her willingness to remain open during the most challenging transitions of her life that revealed new possibilities. "God works in mysterious ways, through people and circumstances," she shares. "I was now the "yes girl" and saying yes to everything that was showing up. If someone invited me to an event I was all in," she adds. She was open to new messages and she didn't want to miss out. "You never know who is going to cross your path or what new relationship you're going to develop," she shares. She knew that new ideas are often presented to you when you get out of your comfort zone and interact with others.

It seems that her entire past had beautifully unfolded and set her up for the fabulous journey she now experiences everyday. She is able to reflect in the wonder of every obstacle and crossroads that she faced. She unlocked her faith and her heart in a new and profound way that attracted greatness. She believes the best is yet to come; and when it arrives she'll be ready with arms open wide. Aana loves where she is in her life. Her heart is open wide and full of intentionality. She is awake to her inner-power and strength to manifest her greatest desires.

I asked her, if she could travel back in time what insight would she share with her younger self? She said, "I would remind my younger self to not lose sight in the fact that I was destined for greatness. I was created for something much bigger than I couldn't possibly imagine, see, or know." She adds, "It was as if my future self was actually guiding and lifting me up somehow." She just couldn't see it at the time.

The opportunity that transformed her life, started out as an intuitive feeling. It was a Saturday in December, where she experienced a powerful energy, as if an epic opportunity was about to reveal itself. One month later, the opportunity appeared! On Sunday, January 1, 2012, her church pastor suddenly signalled her out and asked her to stand up. "He had never once, called upon me, so why this day of all days?" In front of the entire congregation, he told her that she was about to receive a deeper calling in her life; and 11 days later she had a meeting with the man that would sponsor her into this new anti-aging company. During my interview with Aana, it seemed that for the fist time, she instantly connected all of the dots and the energies that miraculously conspire to put her on the path of sheer greatness.

Earlier that month, before all this had transpired, and while working in her previous health & wellness company; Aana had prayed everyday for God to send her 100 women, whose lives she could change and whose bodies she could transform. Little did she know, that these 100 women would present themselves as partners, not in her current company, but rather in this new anti-aging business.

Big Dreamers

~ Dream Bit ~
Big Dreamers Are Governed By Bigger Laws
Big Dreamers remain open to powerful, universal laws, to manifest their desires. They feel connected to the energy of everything around them, and hence, they are able to act on the right opportunities that show up in their path.

Aana always discerned at a deeper level that she didn't need to be the smartest or brightest person in the room. What she knew for certain was she could outwork anyone. She recognized her ability to work hard and knew that anything she applied herself to would eventually pay off. When she undertakes meaningful work, driven by purpose, it ignites and unleashes her higher self. This is an energy she values deeply; it drives her actions and attracts people and meaningful opportunities her way. "When I feel connected to a greater outcome, through service to others, I'm able to harness a deeper level of commitment and focus," she shares.

Leading up to 2012, her heart craved a meaningful connection to a deeper purpose. She was craving a soulful collaboration where she could pour all of her love and passion into helping transform people's lives. Looming in the back of her mind was the fear of having to go back to a full-time job though. She hated the thought of being interviewed by women half her age and having to work for someone else! These thoughts motivated her to look up and connect with something bigger than herself.

~ Dream Bit ~
Big Dreamers Choose An Emotion Of Love

Big Dreamers do not allow fear to overcome them. They avoid being high jacked by their emotions. They crush the fear by pouring themselves into creating themselves and their dreams. They embrace deeper levels of love for themselves and for others around them.

She chose to channel her fear, by focusing on the lifestyle she desired to create. She wouldn't let the fear of having to work for someone else over the next 40 years dominant her thoughts. These images activated the creative side of Aana, and she began looking and being more open to creative opportunities that would soon present themselves. She was strong-willed and a crusader on a mission, to dream bigger and create her fabulous life. She wouldn't let the energy of past events and circumstances block her from dreaming big. She knew how to work hard and she was prepared to outwork anyone, especially, if she was given the right opportunity to create something meaningful. She was a strong and independent woman.

She is what I call, "simply fabulous." She inspires everyone around her to release the breaks and pursue a life of independence. She wasn't interested in pouring endless hours towards building someone else's dream. She was driven by a passion to create her own dream and inspired to teach others to do the same.

~ Dream Bit ~

Big Dreamers Are On Fire

Big Dreamers are excited to leap out of bed each morning and invest the time in creating and living their passions. What is the legacy you want to create and what do you wish to be remembered for? Big Dreamers live their passion.

Interestingly enough, this anti-aging opportunity left Aana questioning whether this was the gift that she had been anxiously waiting for. Even though she believed in the power of network marketing, a part of her resisted this opportunity. However, with arms stretched out and up towards the heavens, she was ready to receive the opportunity enabling her to pour her passion and purpose into helping 100 women. "I had only one request of God - make it obvious," she shares.

Throughout this time with Aana, I sensed there was an energy far greater at work, one that surpassed the rational side of her brain. She was intrigued and filled with curiosity for the passion her friend displayed when he presented her with the opportunity. She thought, "He was so excited about this new company that he must know something, I don't!" He was a very astute businessman and she knew that he had done extensive research on the company and the market opportunity. Based on these facts, she was willing to listen with an open mind. She wasn't prepared to go any further than listening, since she was not looking for another network marketing company. Yet, in the back of her mind there was a faint whisper of something that inspired her to pay closer attention. "When my friend showed me the presentation, it was the before and after pictures that truly inspired me to try the product," she recalls. Further to that, she thought, "if I'm this excited about trying the product, won't millions of other people get just as excited as me?" Her friend made his presentation and simply left her with a bottle of night cream to sample for the next five days. After her friend left she sat there and contemplated what just transpired. She remembers thinking, "he simply got excited, shared some information, showed me before and after pictures; before leaving me with a bottle to sample - anybody can do this. If anyone can do this, it would duplicate." She also thought, "Can this be the opportunity that I've been praying for?"

She couldn't get the simplicity of what just transpired out of her mind. She was expecting a convoluted business pitch from her friend. She was used to creating complex infrastructure in business. Yet, here was a man, she trusted and knew to be successful at what he did; and his overall presentation to her was so fabulously simple!

For three days, she thought of nothing else. She loved the product and felt a surge of inspiring energy igniting the Big Dreamer within. She'd been praying for an opportunity, and she was now presented with what she believed could be the next big thing. She remembers, "All I thought was, how could I let this opportunity pass me by?"

After three sleepless nights, she went online, did a bit more research on the company, and decided to buy a $1,000 business pack. She already maxed out her credit card so she was unsure, if the transaction would even go through. "I made it a test for myself, if it didn't go through, then I knew it was not meant to be," she recalls. She was prepared to close the laptop and walk away, but to her surprise, she was approved and officially enrolled as a brand partner, in this exciting, new anti-aging company. "I couldn't believe it, I was baffled," she recounted. "This payment should not have gone through, so it must have been fate."

As she sat at her desk, in deep reflection on her life journey, a memory of her pastor, asking her to stand up instantly flashed in her mind. Looking out the window, she saw herself with arms stretched wide, looking out onto the ocean and praying to the heavens above. It was as if time had suddenly collided. All of the past challenges and events that transpired in her life, miraculously brought her to this place. "Everything just felt right and in complete alignment," she remembers.

When her anti-aging business pack arrived a few days later, she immediately handed out the bottles to 10 of her friends to sample. After seeing nine of her friends experience incredible results she knew this was the real deal! Her belief in this product was rock solid. Interestingly enough, 9 out of 10 friends who first experienced the amazing results didn't even purchase the product or join her business. "It was at that point where I almost decided to quit this business," she recounted. "I used to care what people thought, until I tried to pay my bills with their thoughts," she adds.

~ Dream Bit ~

Big Dreamers Aren't Influenced By Others

Big Dreamers don't allow dream stealers to influence the direction of their lives. They listen to their inner-voice and allow it to guide their actions. They share and tell their story with no expectation. They develop themselves daily in order to discipline their disappointment.

Aana Camp's Top Actions for Dreaming Bigger:

- Create a vision board in vivid detail with words, phrases and pictures of the life you desire to create.
- Align what you see visually with the dreams of your fabulous future.
- Spend a few moments everyday visualizing and feel the feelings of having what you are seeking.
- Create and shout out daily affirmations for the life you're creating. An affirmation begins with the words "I am..." and "It's a proven fact that neurologists have determined that the speech centre in our brains have more power and influence on every cell and neuron in our bodies," she shares.
- Reprogram your sub conscious mind by replacing negative thoughts with powerful and positive statements.

- Carve out the time every day to live inspired actions no matter how busy you are. Turn off the TV and commit yourself to replacing the distractions with only positive and life changing activities.

- Write out your goals in greater detail for all areas of your life. Take action everyday towards reaching them. Write out your goals with an expectation of reaching them in 5 years. "One of my goals that kick-started my reinvention was to achieve a new physical level of health and vitality. I knew I needed to be in top shape to have the energy to build fast." She also created and implemented powerful discipline and actions to reach her goals. "One of my powerful goals was that my husband David and I would have the financial means to travel freely anywhere in the world," she shares. "We will cultivate extraordinary friends in 5 new countries that we would visit with often. All of these goals that I had written down, planned and acted on, were all realized by 2015," she adds.

Aana was working 50-60 hour weeks while starting her new network marketing business. Her success didn't come easily, but rather as a result of her deep desire to invent herself. She committed herself, every free minute she had to visualizing and shouting out her affirmations for success. She fixated on her dreams and wouldn't let anyone sway her off course. She believed in herself and in her passion to create something meaningful in other people's lives. She avoided distractions, by taking on only the actions that would generate powerful momentum and nurture her craft. She empowered others to follow her. It was her burning desire to cultivate these new behaviours that transformed her into attracting greater opportunities. She reprogrammed and reconditioned her mind for success.

She was determined and became highly disciplined in the formation of greater success habits, which eventually transformed her, her son's, and the lives of thousands of other people. Aana is the ultimate role model and epitomizes the qualities of a Big Dreamer. She anchored herself to her vision and didn't stop until she achieved every one of her goals. She continued to plough ahead, always focused on the end goal. She lives her life with grace, authenticity, passion and purpose.

Aana lives with a newfound belief that she possesses a power that can radiate outwards. She recognizes, at a cellular level, her belief in her own abilities to inspire profound change in others. She has an optimistic outlook of channelling this positive energy into thousands of people around her. She lives with great intention and hope for others. She shares, "when others allow my belief to infuse them, it helps transform their lives." She wants others to trust in her belief and follow her path, knowing that together they will change the world, by first changing themselves. She wants be remembered for living a fabulous and zestful life. She wants to be regarded, as being trustworthy, reliable; and know that everyone she poured her energy into mattered.

I believe she will be remembered as someone that inspired the masses to become a better version of themselves. She dedicates this chapter to her son, Skylar. In her words to him she notes, "I want you to remember me for being a courageous woman that gracefully seized every fabulous experience that life had to offer. I hope you remember me for being the best mom in the world, who listened to you and believed in you, long before you believed in yourself. I want you to feel that you were supported in everything you pursued, and see me as an inspiring role model for you. I love you Skylar."

Aana lives today in Southern California and is living her dream life, happily married to her husband and the love of her life, David.

~ *A Dedication to my mom by Skylar Perkins* ~

Wow, how blessed am I to have such an incredible role model in my life! How inspiring to have a mentor that's gone out there, paved the way, and shown me what's necessary to have success at such a high level. It's one thing to hear someone talk about their path to greatness, but it's another to have been given the opportunity to physically watch a person, transform into their highest potential. Ever since I can remember, she's not just been a hard worker, but more importantly, she's been committed to constant growth on a daily basis– something that I see a lot of adults stop striving towards. I'm so proud to call her mom and I honestly couldn't think of anyone on this planet who would be a better role model!

99

Photography by: Omero Guerrero

4. Brittany Burtz
The <u>WAY</u> Through WHY

"My wish for the world is that every person remain curious and open to explore what it means to believe at a greater level, so that they can begin to live their passion, their purpose and their gifts with more love and fulfillment than ever before." ~ Brittany Burtz

A Dedication to my Mom, Cindy

"It was your belief in me, my entire life, especially as a child. Your unconditional love was the purest love that I could ever experience. You saw me for who I am, at the deepest level, even before I ever saw myself. No matter what hardships I had experienced in my life, you would leave me love notes everywhere. You would affirm to me, all of the things you loved about me. You created my ability to dream even bigger. You amplified my ability to love unconditionally every single day."

Brittany Burtz *exists* to inspire the world through a new way of being, that once sourced and lived will elevate each person individually and collectively. Her early years were filled with tremendous joy, love and laughter. As a child, she exuded happiness everywhere she went. This was her essence. She was the kind of girl that would hug a complete stranger in a grocery store. She was filled with a deeper curiosity for how the world worked. Her grandmother would often comment that she could never sit still. She was always exploring and experiencing her environment. She went about her days wide-eyed and filled with unbridled curiosity for the colourful world that surrounded her.

An awareness of her deeper self started as early as preschool. It was around this time when she began taking notice of the different polarities of her external environment. It was in preschool at 4-years-old when Brittany first started to question things in her universe. "Why did that happen and why did that person do that to me, were questions that entered my mind," she recalls. She was deeply impacted with the behaviours that she witnessed while playing in the school playground. She questioned why certain kids would pull pranks on her. She thought, "what drove these kids to act towards me in this manner?"

At the time, she never judged these kids, she understood that they were oblivious to their actions and their behaviour was most likely attributed to copying other kids in the playground. Still, these observations perplexed this curious little mind. "Why would these kids want to say hurtful things to me, I'm such a good person," she adds.

Brittany was able to observe and learn from these younger years and her awareness today is a result of years of personal development, and from being open to insights from some of her greatest spiritual teachers. She approaches every challenging situation by not condemning the other person, but rather separating and distinguishing the unconscious behaviour from the person. It's this ability to separate the behaviour that helps her live with greater fulfillment. She is able to look back throughout her years and gain a richer perspective by looking through and around the behaviour of others in order to see the *real* person inside.

Her ability to notice, what she defines as "polarity", continued throughout her earlier education. She was picked on extensively by, what she thought at the time, were her trusted friends. "These were my closest friends that I spent most of my time with, so why would they say and do such hurtful things to me," she shares. She had a real passion for art that started around the age of eight. She shares an emotional memory with me, as to how she created a beautiful piece of art for a Grade 4 contest. "I was so excited and I decided to draw a tiger and a lion," she recounts. Brittany was so proud of the work that she had created. One of her friends was the judge of this contest and Brittany recalls how a group of friends casted her drawing aside, rejecting it purposefully, in front of her. This was traumatic to Brittany. She was so hurt by these friends and their intention of making her feel sad.

This kind of behaviour seemed to follow Brittany into her high school years. Interestingly enough she takes 100% responsibility for the behaviour in her life though. What started as early as grade 4, planted a seed of self-doubt in her mind. This led to growing feelings of insecurity that never existed in this loving child prior to her early education. A deeper need for external validation was growing below the surface and manifested later on in her teens. "This need to be liked by other people never entered my consciousness in my early years," she shares. She just assumed that everyone loved her, since she, herself was nothing but loving to others.

Big Dreamers Drive Their Behaviour

Big Dreamers see everyone trying to do their best within their own state of consciousness. They rise above every situation by focusing on the learning in any given moment. When faced with a challenging energy they pause in the moment and ask: "What am I meant to learn from this person or this situation?"

These younger and curious years implanted a deeper awareness in her mind of the different polarities that exist all around us. In her early years, she added meaning to these negative situations, which turned into repressed negative emotions and limiting beliefs that surfaced later on in life; and affected her personal relationships. This deep and internal need to be liked, accepted and validated by people, created a greater sense of shyness, insecurity and fear inside of her. She turned to the power of personal development to overcome these emotions though and is in a much greater place today.

~ Dream Bit ~

Big Dreamers Don't Let The Past Control Them

Big Dreamers don't let emotions of the past control the present moment. They look for the teaching in every situation through personal development. They focus their energy into defining themselves in the present and avoid directing unnecessary energy to past events.

Brittany was always a Big Dreamer. Her earlier years were flooded with thoughts of where and who she wanted to be. Her view of the world was expansive and limitless. In high school, she faced greater challenges that seemed to baffle her ability to dream bigger, however. It was during her sophomore year, that she was pressured to identify a career. At that time, it seemed to her that she would choose what spoke to her soul. Her passion was art and she had a long-held desire of becoming an artist. "I wanted to create art everyday, for the rest of my life," she remembers. She imagined attending world-class art openings and witnessing others travelling from far-away places to appreciate her art. Brittany was astonished as to how everyone else in her class selected careers that seemed more logical, safer and conservative. The people that Brittany looked up to in her life, shared with her that she could not exist as an artist. "The people closest to me were basically telling me, I couldn't live my dreams, and make a career from my passions," she recounted.

Listening to Brittany, I'm reminded of a powerful Big Dreamer, the late Steve Jobs, co-founder of Apple. In one of his earlier interviews, he spoke to the power of passion, and said *if you're not passionate about what you do, you won't be able to push through the difficult times and you'll ultimately quit.* I love this! We have to love what we do and it's as simple as that.

I'm also reminded of Napoleon Hill's book titled, *Think and Grow Rich.* One only has to read this book to see the insight of Steve Jobs truly come to life. Napoleon Hill spent 20 years of his life interviewing some of the most passionate inventors and entrepreneurs, like, Dale Carnegie and Thomas Edison. Each of these people commonly shared a burning desire and passion for changing the world. As a human species, aren't we meant to ignite and live our passion? We tap into our passion, when we feel good and experience tremendous joy.

As an inspirational speaker, I'm baffled by how many people in my audiences don't know what they are passionate about. It doesn't help that our school systems do very little, if anything, to ignite and encourage living through our passions. So, it's not surprising to me, that Brittany experienced this kind of energy in her high school years. Only through living an existence of greater passion, will you have the power to create more meaningful outcomes in your life.

Think about what you are seeking. In my previous book titled, *I Don't Know What the Hell I'm Doing®,* I share an insight called: "simplify", so that you can clear the space to ignite and live your passion.

We arrive in this world as a blank canvas of pure potentiality. Then somewhere between the age of 4 and 40, we allow this canvas to become stained with external perceptions and by what others think we should be or do with our life. We suppress our passions and in doing so, we lose the connection to who we really are and to our inner being. We choose a path that others want for us. The outcome sadly, is that we end up creating a world of unhappy and unfulfilled doers. We become defined by objects, careers and job titles, and lose sight of what truly brings us joy. Months turn into years, and eventually, decades have passed us by and we are left with stuff that doesn't fulfill us. We then look outside of ourselves by placing the blame for our unhappiness on the external world. It's far easier to choose others to blame than doing the work on ourselves and taking 100% responsibility for the path and the life we've created.

We are born as human beings not human doings. While action is required, it's living with greater passion that ignites our fulfillment.

We are born as Big Dreamers and perhaps it's time we turn our dream machine back on, because when we do, we will be living with joy and the world will be a better place.

~ Dream Bit ~

Big Dreamers Do Only Things That Bring Them Joy

Big Dreamers live through their passions everyday and inspire others with their contagious enthusiasm. If your passion excites you it will influence all of your actions. Your passion is your GPS continuously aligning you with your inner being. It casts a light on your desired path by showing you how and where to go.

Brittany was being told at an impressionable age that she wouldn't be able to generate income from living her passions. Her closest friends advised her to choose an education that would lead to a "real job" in the future. So, that day in her sophomore year, with the pressure from others she made an unconscious decision and chose architecture as her career path. Although, she had a curiosity for architecture, this choice was not in alignment with her passion for existing as a global artist. Architecture was not her true art.

She did what society said she should do though. Brittany left home at the age of 18 and enrolled in college. She had an optimistic outlook on this new adventure, and attending college sparked a whole new series of awakenings. One of her deeper realizations was recognizing the polarity between who she was inside, compared to her surroundings. Most of her associations at the time were people that were heavy into the party scene, and Brittany felt torn between these worlds. A year into college another realization surfaced and her initial excitement for newfound independence, quickly transcended into a deep sense of unhappiness. These feelings and moments of melancholy influenced Brittany to spend time reflecting on her own. More and more, she found herself disconnecting from her friends. This deeper reflection revealed that something just wasn't right. "I wasn't feeling as happy as I knew I could be," she recalls.

She found peace in driving along the Pacific Coast Highway, from Long Beach State where she attended College to Laguna Beach. This quiet time alone grounded her. It re-ignited her ability to believe in herself and in her bigger dreams. Being alone, helped her reflect and feel everything in her life. This phase of deep contemplation carried on for months. With her feet in the sand and eyes wide-open, looking out into the ocean, she began imaging a new life. Her days were filled with reading, drinking tea, and intuitively asking herself questions.

It wasn't just the car that was driving her; there was something spiritually accelerating her intuition. Brittany hadn't yet discovered the world of personal development nor had she attracted mentors. "I felt as if I was uncovering something deeper about myself, that I intuitively knew would one day become a new way of being for me," she shares. She would ask, "who am I meant to be and what is next for me? At the time, I didn't realize the power that these kinds of questions can have like I do now," she recounted. These deeper questions helped her sort through the emotions she was experiencing. I love the energy in the power of a question and its ability to stop us in our tracks. It's one of the reasons why I wrote and published a

Big Dreamers

book series called: *THINQ, Live the Question.* It's the bigger questions that truly reveal the answers that our hearts are seeking.

By living through this creative process, that asks bigger questions, invites answers, and carves out time for deeper reflection, Brittany opened herself up to new possibilities. She recalls a vivid memory of the night that changed everything. To deal with sadness or emotions that were occurring in her life, she would often leave her apartment and walk in nature. It was the act of being outside, driving, walking along the beach, or just getting a cup of tea, that grounded her in the present moment. It was this one night, where she recounts feeling a greater sense of unease within herself. It was this energy that represented a kind of pull, a tug of war feeling, which often occurs when our inner being is speaking to us.

~ Dream Bit ~
Big Dreamers Listen To Their Inner Voice

Big Dreamers go within and listen to their inner voice. They are aware of their intuitive gifts and they harness this energy. They reflect and live big questions knowing the answers are whispers from the universe. They meditate daily recognizing that the *how* will reveal itself when they trust and let go.

She decided to go to dinner on her own, followed by a long and contemplative walk on the beach. Brittany's surroundings and her associations at this point in life were not lifting her up or magnifying her. She felt there was something else calling her that would bring her a greater sense of joy. "What is next and what is coming for me, were the thoughts that filled my mind, as I walked along the boardwalk that night," she shares. A man named Brad suddenly appeared. She noticed him from a far, working as an airbrush tattoo artist. Brittany laughingly recounts, how this unplanned interaction with Brad, became a defining moment and a gift from the universe.

It was in that moment, that a higher power answered her call. She felt deeply connected and compelled to share what was in her heart with this man. She experienced a deep sense of trust, growing inside of her, and after a couple of hours he asked her to consider joining him at an event he was attending later that week. He shared with her that it was an assemblage of inspiring people.

This event served as Brittany's first exposure to the entrepreneurial world. Brad's energy roused her interest and curiosity. She was intrigued and open to the idea of earning extra money on the side while she was attending college. She was also ready to open herself up to new levels of fulfillment and connection in her life. At the age of 19, she was baffled with the stories and energy presenters were sharing. She was astonished with this new world of self-exploration and personal mastery. It was as if the universe suddenly chimed in and she was on fire to develop herself mentally and spiritually. This world roused her long-held desire for deeper levels of self-awareness. She now found herself questioning the merits of formal education and this defining moment, became the catalyst for her exponential growth years later.

~ Dream Bit ~

Big Dreamers Are Open To The Energies Of Synchronicity

Big Dreamers recognize the synchronicities of pivotal events and trust and embrace them.

They move throughout the world with a sense of grace, confidence and openness.

They learn how to replace the fear, with love, for they learn to love themselves.

She was astonished by her instant shift from fear and uncertainty to one of clarity and inner peace. It was in those moments that answers began flowing to her, and she simply had to listen with her heart. People, resources and opportunities suddenly began revealing themselves and later that year, she met a great mentor, who connected her to other extraordinary people. Suddenly, her world was a shimmering haven. Her life was inundated with positivity and uplifting information, encouragement and growth.

Shortly after these events, she decided leaving college was the right thing to do. Her initial reasons for attending college no longer aligned with the person she was becoming. In the past, others told her what she should do in order to secure a job and a career. She thought she wanted security in her life and that a college degree would lead her there. "If I did that, I was doing what my family wanted me to do," she adds. However, through her journey of self-education, she was able to uncover the deeper meaning behind the unconscious choices she made in her earlier years.

These new revelations and feelings of self-empowerment influenced her decision to leave college. The Big Dreamer was ignited more than ever. She believed that this new journey of self-development would help her manifest her dreams. She knew she was a creator and could manifest anything that she focused on. Her new way of being was beginning to emerge within her mind. It expanded new levels of growth and knowledge that she now believed would not be accessible from formal education alone. "At the time, if I felt that my dreams could have been fulfilled with a college education, then I certainly would have pursued it," she shares. "Other factors were now igniting my passion though, such as creating financial freedom through owning my own business…and I could now see myself living my passions through my creativity and my art," she adds. This way of being, filled Brittany's heart and soul. She imagined living with greater levels of happiness, bliss and fulfillment.

~ Dream Bit ~
Big Dreamers Believe They Are Co-Creators

Big Dreamers are born as co-creators and feel guided by a stronger creative process. They master this energy by believing their dream is possible and taking powerful actions through inspired thoughts to receive these gifts with tremendous levels of gratitude.

I asked Brittany what the impact on her family felt like, after she shared her decision to quit college. She paused for a moment then began to share that this was definitely one of the most challenging times in her life. Her family didn't comprehend her decision to leave college. They were profoundly opposed with her decision. Ultimately, it led to a disconnection and much needed separation with her family. Brittany had an exalted mission to immerse herself into personal development. She attended training seminars and surrounded herself with inspiring and supportive mentors. These inspired actions helped her navigate a sea of uncomfortable discussions with her family. Her mom meant the world to her, and she loved her dad and her sister so much. "It was difficult to have so much confrontation and disagreement during those times," she recounted. She was hurt and misunderstood. She could only imagine that her parents felt the same way. This was not a happy time for their family. Looking back, she regrets not having the personal development tools to more effectively respond to her family.

It was a roller coaster of emotions. Like any 19 year old, she was angry, frustrated and resentful. She expresses regret for the things she said and did at the time. Recounting these earlier times, she never would have displayed that kind of energy towards her family. The new path that Brittany wanted to blaze was not aligned with the path her parents set out for her. This misalignment of values only caused disconnection, hurt and sadness within her family. Despite this, she had an optimistic outlook and pursued the most significant changes in her life, by growing and becoming a better version of herself. "I was pursuing my dream, not my parent's, and for that reason it's easy to see why they felt a sense of abandonment," she adds. Even though her family was close to her they didn't understand Brittany's new levels of awareness for what was truly possible. At the time, her family was unaware of the calling and the purpose that was growing in her heart, and what she desired to create. Her family was baffled as to how to respond, so they instead, projected their feelings of what they believed was best for her. "I know that my parents loved me so much, and through this love, they

113

still projected what they wanted for me, instead of listening to what was in my heart," she adds.

This disconnection with her family was a necessity at the time. Although she experienced deep sadness and loss, she didn't allow her emotions to consume her. She chose to immerse herself into personal development; and chose to be surrounded and uplifted by the new positive leaders and mentors in her life. This energy and support helped her stay the course. These mentors lived, what Brittany wanted to model and experience in her own life. They supported, encouraged and rallied around her and became her support structure.

~ Dream Bit ~
Big Dreamers Don't Rely On Their Family To Support Their Bigger Dreams
Big Dreamers recognize the ones we love the most are often our greatest teachers. They frequently give us the most ridicule and opposition when we are about to make a change in our lives.

I asked Brittany what she would say to her younger self, given the chance. She paused with deep reflection, as if she was actually being transported back in time to meet with the 19-year-old version of herself. As she began to speak, I sensed a deep connection to her higher self, which I believe, she intuitively experienced during her younger years. There is no doubt, that Brittany understands this power that we all posses, this inner knowing of our higher purpose. With every breath, a now wiser Brittany, shares a deeper compassion for what her family endured. It's as if, she could feel the hurt, they experienced. "I would help my younger self understand that my parents loved me unconditionally, and this was their way of showing their love. I would tell myself, to understand the hurt they felt, and not take it personally since the hurt had nothing to do with me," she adds. She added that she would help her younger self understand, at a deeper level, the pain that her parents lived. "I would tell my younger self to honour my parents' state of mind, and know they were doing their best," she shares. I admire her energy in this moment, as if she's actually placing her hand on her younger self's heart. "There is something so special about following your own heart," she adds. She would want her younger self to share from her heart and ask her parents if they would honour her choice to pursue her own way, knowing and respecting that it's not their way. I love how Brittany poses a thoughtful question to her younger self, "Just ask them...just ask them with love," she continues, "would they support you, knowing this was a calling you feel deep in your heart, even if they don't understand it?"

~ **Dream Bit** ~

Big Dreamers Lead From The Heart

Big Dreamers focus on sharing the outcomes they wish others to experience. They understand the power of intention and its ability to create more meaningful connections in their lives. It's letting go of expectations from others that will lighten the load in your life.

I admire this young woman. She lives and acts through her heart. "Sometimes those closest to us, only need to energetically support your calling in the world," she shares. Her message is one of love and greater acceptance of others. Quite often, those closest to us, don't understand the decisions we make, or they don't show up the way we would like them to. These kinds of expectations create frustration, and can impact our ability to open our hearts. Living with expectations closes us off from realizing our potential. It only perpetuates the disconnection between others and ourselves. Sometimes, it's more important to create the conditions within our lives to share from a place of pure love and understanding.

Imagine a world, where we could all learn how to listen from a place of non-judgment. Imagine the peace that would resonate throughout the world, eliminating conflict as a result of misunderstandings. This is a world and an energy that Brittany has created within herself and inspires in others. I love how she shares with her younger self, to love her parents where they are at and continue focusing on what she is creating for herself. "Surround yourself with positive people that lift you up and help you stay the course, and eventually know, that your family will come around and experience the truth in who you become, and that you made the right choice," she adds.

Look back on to your own life and the energy surrounding some of your most challenging conflicts, what were you feeling in the moment? Was it rejection, frustration, anger, hurt, a lack of compassion? Now, think of how you felt 24 hours later. How many of those emotions actually survived? These are all emotions that are driven by fear. All we really want as human beings is to be felt as if we are being heard. We all want to feel as if our life mattered. We want to feel a sense of contribution, especially to our children's lives.

Big Dreamers

These are some of the emotions that Brittany's family was experiencing. She wasn't trying to hurt anyone, she was simply following her heart, and what she believed was her deeper calling. She was passionate about self-development and was inspired to create a new way of being. She became awake and aware to new possibilities, as a result of being open and on track with her dreams. This is the power behind never giving up on your dreams. Once you recognize that not everyone has to get you, join you or show up the way you wish they would; you will experience a dramatic shift in all areas of your life.

~ Dream Bit ~

Big Dreamers Are Never Defeated

Big Dreamers don't allow themselves to become hijacked by their emotions. By focusing on their creative energy, they propel themselves forward instead of remaining fixed in one place. They are never defeated and see rejection as a part of their success momentum.

What started Brittany down a path of dreaming big was a process called, "dream building." She chose to surround herself with like-minded, Big Dreamers, and that energy magnified her passions and desires. Sometimes, that's all it takes to kick-start your dream building to align your energy with positive people.

In my earlier years, when I decided to exist as an inspiration to others, I needed to seek out and surround myself, with new and positive people. I created a circle of Big Dreamers, and met with them two times per month. Eventually, that circle grew in size and I branded it as, *The Tank®,* which became evenings of inspired thinking. What's interesting is that these inspired evenings went on to inspire thousands of people across Canada. The dream building process is powerful. It ignites your passion and your purpose helping you decide what you want most in life. You can start anywhere, and at any age, but you need to start!

Dream building is fun and simple. Start with writing out the things that you want to experience most in your life. Then, cut out some visuals that bring your list to life, and compile it onto a vision board, creating a graphical representation of what you want. Share the energy of this vision board with those closest to you. Then create a daily ritual to experience and soak in the energy of it. Every morning, upon waking up look at it, close your eyes, take it all in, and feel yourself living your dream life. See yourself being transported into that vision board, being and doing all of the things on it. As you go about your day, carve out 20-30 min to focus on some actions that keeps your dream alive. It's not enough to create a vision board once and never look at it again. The key is to build up momentum and keep your dream alive.

Next, get a gratitude journal, and every night write out the 3-5 things that you are most grateful for; knowing that with every thought, belief and action you are moving yourself closer to realizing your dreams. It doesn't take a quantum leap to reach the end goal. What will bring you greater fulfillment in your life is carving out the space and setting the intention to live your dream everyday. For me, it's about loving the journey and seeking out other Big Dreamers, like Brittany, who I was meant to shine a light on.

This is what we can learn from these Big Dreamers and their stories published in this book. They made a conscious decision, to get onto their path, not someone else's, but their own. Everyday, they are growing bit by bit. They condition their mind in order to generate the thoughts that attract and open us up to inspired actions. Some actions are only 20 minutes a day, like sharing your opportunity; while other actions, are defining moments, like attracting a mentor at a meeting. Whatever it may be, Big Dreamers, like Brittany, live for the moment with great intention, gratitude, passion and purpose. They wake up hungry to start the day and move through life with intensity and determination. They say no to thousands of distractions, and protect themselves from the negativity of the world, through personal development.

What I admire about Brittany is her willingness and openness to listen to her heart. This energy aligns her actions with her inner being. She takes 100% responsibility to create and live her dreams. She has developed an immense capacity to savour the simple things in life, such as writing, creating, nurturing and inspiring others. She has faced challenging forks in the road, and has seen every situation, and everyone as a brilliant teacher. She has learned through great wisdom how to be the moment. Brittany is without a doubt a Big Dreamer, and the world is only beginning to experience her passion and purpose.

Along her journey, there were many struggles, she faced. It wasn't all sunshine and roses. There were emotional challenges she faced in her relationships and the financial pressures her and her boyfriend endured; exerted a ton of stress on her ability to dream big.

"We were almost evicted from our apartment and had our car repossessed," she adds. At times, their diet consisted of eating rice and beans. Many days were a struggle just to buy food. Brittany and her boyfriend did whatever they could to survive. There was a period of time they experienced a full meal only when she went back home or a friend paid. Her mom didn't know at the time what her daughter was experiencing and for years, Brittany hid these financial pressures from her family.

Strong willed though, she never let a shortage of money stop her from visualizing a bigger future. One of her consistent, "dream building" actions, was driving through million dollar neighbourhoods and imagining that she lived there. Brittany never let the reality and pain of her current circumstances stop her from surrounding herself with extraordinary and successful mentors. She never focused on what she didn't have, but rather, on the energy of where she was going. She just kept building and adding to her vision board pictures of the life she desired to create. Her vision board was filled with the places that she would visit, the homes and the lifestyle she would create, and the great mentors she would surround herself with.

~ Dream Bit ~

Big Dreamers Develop The Quality Of Their Minds

Big Dreamers know that money and finances are a concept that starts in the mind.
To change anything in life first change the quality and state of your mind.

She was a crusader with an optimistic outlook on life. She experienced her dream lifestyle, clearly in her mind, and felt it in her cells. She wanted to instil her belief deeply into her unconscious mind. She believed this energy wouldn't come from college classrooms, a high school aptitude test or pre-selected careers. She knew, that to dream big, it had to start with a deeper inner reflection of who she wanted to be. She modelled her mentors. She didn't let herself get stuck by the lack of progress. She focused her energy on what she was visualizing for her future self. She comprehended the power of dreaming big. She nurtured her dreams and cultivated her relationships with greater intensity. Brittany knew that she possessed the power to change her current reality and define a new one.

~ Dream Bit ~

Big Dreamers Focus Only On Success

Big Dreamers focus on expanding their world.

They displace thoughts of worry and fear with love and prosperity.

They surround themselves with highly successful people.

121

"By surrounding myself with powerful mentors it raised my vibration and helped flow greater thoughts of prosperity into my life," she recounted. Asking successful people questions and listening with the intent to understand opens doors for a different reality and a different future. During her childhood years, Brittany made a choice on how to perceive her world, and this became the start of her creative process to manifesting her dreams. By flexing and conditioning her dreaming muscles, she nurtured a new foundation for success. This didn't just happen it was through her willingness to change her circumstances that influenced her to set a powerful intention for the life she desired to create.

However, what was showing up in her life, for many years, was the exact opposite of the life that she craved to manifest. "It didn't feel good to experience life and the hardships we were facing," shares an emotional Brittany. "I didn't like that I couldn't eat healthy and buy the organic foods that my body was craving," she recounts. Living with higher levels of health and nutrition is something that Brittany values deeply. Today she is filled with tremendous gratitude for the ability to live and afford this state of being everyday. The most painful memories were from when she would walk into a grocery store and cry, almost every time, for having to buy non-healthy food, because it was a lot less expensive. While walking down the aisles, Brittany used the power of visualization, her most powerful mind tool, and saw her grocery cart filled to the top with only the healthiest foods. She saw in her future, her shopping at places, like *Whole Foods*, and not worrying about price tags.

It was through cultivating a more powerful mind that elevated the only thing that was in her control, her ability to overcome and control her thoughts. The art of visualization is still her greatest tool and constantly driving her to ignite her bigger dreams.

~ Dream Bit ~

Big Dreamers Flex Their Visualization Muscles

Big Dreamers push beyond the pain. They fail and fail again, eventually turning their failures into significant wins.

They see through the discomfort by employing the art of visualization.

Brittany's visualization consisted of seeing where she would live and what her surroundings would feel like. She imagined her ideal physique and living a healthy and vibrant lifestyle. She imagined, being surrounded by tremendous love and support everyday. "Before anything physically showed up in my life, it all started in my mind, through powerful visualization," she adds.

Today, she harnesses a new level of confidence and certainty seems to resonate from every cell in her body. The future potential and possibility that now awaits her is limitless. She believes that anything she desires to experience will become a reality.

Brittany is excited about the expanse of her future, knowing and believing in herself and in her capacity to create extraordinary experiences. She believes that all of her past tools, successes and the people she attracted, prepared her for what's truly possible. "I believe that for the rest of my existence here, I can create and have whatever it is I desire, as long as it is in alignment with my highest and greatest good," she adds.

She exists to create a world that starts within. A world that is filled with love, devotion, authenticity, balance, and giving to others. She imagines a world where we exist at a higher vibration. "I know this kind of energy will transcend happiness into the world," she adds. Her long-held desire is to become a model of possibility for others. It is through this new way of being that she hopes to induce a ripple effect that will be experienced and practiced daily by others. "It will ignite within every human being and will last for eternity; spanning far and wide," shares Brittany. It's an energy and a frequency that has always been there, ready to be sourced and realized in the world," she adds. There is a global power in this kind of deep connectivity and connection of the human race. Brittany loves the person she has become and says she is, "a being, with a sense of awe and wonder."

Her deeper curiosity has existed within for her entire life. She has continually worked at nurturing it and keeping it alive. It's this energy of awe and wonder that inspires her existence. "It is the precursor to everything, growth, giving to others, living with passion and with greater love," shares Brittany. Through this new way of being, she is able to see and experience the inspiration, the beauty and the love in everything all the time. The inspired outcome is an energy filled with greater levels of peace and fulfillment.

Big Dreamers

~ Dream Bit ~
Big Dreamers Never Stop Driving Their Curiosity

Big Dreamers never stop dreaming and imagining possibility. They are curious and live with awe and wonder. They want the best for others and believe in forging a new and inspired connection, within the human race.

Creating this book and spending time with Brittany reminds me of the world I always imagined creating - a world inspired. Imagine a new ROI for the world, one where we all Reach Out and Inspire other Big Dreamers! What new innovations could we create? Imagine replacing a world of fear with one of pure and unconditional love. This energy is what the world needs now, more than ever.

Towards the end of our time together, I asked Brittany if she was having fun and she joyfully responded, "yes!" When I asked her why this was so much fun, she expressed her vision and desire for millions of people to feel this way everyday.

The sounds of nature chimed in as Brittany paused to contemplate the final question of our interview. I asked her to imagine, thousands of people attending her funeral, each holding a copy of this book and reading this chapter. I asked her to share with me how she wants to be remembered. What would she want others to say about the greater impact that she had on the world? She responded, "I want to be remembered for being so happy and experiencing myself and my life with openness and new levels of love and appreciation. I hope that the ones I touched, felt peace within themselves and unconditional love," she concludes.

~ A Dedication from Brittany's father, Kevin Burtz ~

From the time she was born I thought that Brittany was a special soul. I know, all parents feel something kindred to that, but maybe it was because of the special circumstance that I actually got to deliver her and pulled her into this world while her Mother heroically did her part.

At a very early age there was calmness, a serenity about her and a sweetness that was very evident. It was clear this was someone with a very open heart, free of malice, and her Mother did a great job of nurturing a caring attitude.

Brittany always seemed to me to have a sense of curiosity and wonder and I tried to instil in her a desire to explore and learn. I stressed to her one of the lessons my Mother had shared with me, that you can learn anything if you learn to read and how that can open the entire world to you! I thank God that she listened and believe it has served her well in her research, collection of knowledge and growth. I know she still has a ferocious appetite for reading.

Brittany was always a great observer of life around her and observing patterns in that life and taking time to appreciate all aspects of it. When she was quite young I remember us sitting in the backyard many late afternoons and watching large groups of crows flying back down from the mountains to the valleys from where they had come and her realizing that it happened at the same time each day and pondering what had their day been like and where were they going together? I think it was her curiosity and caring that made her a great observer of the human condition and becoming purpose driven in changing herself and others!

The person Brittany has become and what she has accomplished makes me very proud but does not surprise me. Although she has exceeded all I could have wished for her, I know her journey continues as she continues to grow, learn, affect and inspire so many including myself. I can't wait to see where that takes her!

I am proud to be her father and grateful to call her my friend!

BELIEF, ACTION AND FAITH IGNITES THE WAY.

~ Gerry Visca

5. Aaron Dinh
BELIEVE

"I define freedom as breaking away from how society would have you live. With greater success, you are able to inspire others, to be the best version of themselves." ~ Aaron Dinh

Aaron Dinh *exists* to inspire others to be the best version of themselves. He was around 3 years old when his family immigrated to the United States. He was unaware of the significant challenges his family experienced along their journey. As a young boy, he witnessed how hard his family worked just to survive. He was the youngest of three siblings and he developed a strong sense of independence with his parents having to work long hours to support their family. "I always felt I was different and that my family didn't fully understand me. I saw the world in a completely different way," he recounts. His parents were very traditional and they attempted to instil in Aaron the need to focus on school, get good grades and a good job. However, that was not his path. There was a different desire igniting in him, even at an early age.

As a young boy, he rarely asked his parents for toys or money, because he saw how hard they worked and how much they struggled for their family. Seeing the hardships his parents experienced, shaped and strengthened his independent nature. When Aaron reached the age of 15, he started working anywhere that would take him, mostly fast food restaurants and retail jobs. The kind of work didn't matter to him, as he was so focused on earning his own way in life. He found himself moving, from job to job and his burning independence was growing stronger everyday.

Unlike Aaron, his siblings chose to live at home and attend school in order to further their education. At the time, Aaron felt responsible for creating his own way and had a strong desire to be independent. Leading up to college, Aaron had worked at over 30 different types of jobs. His family often criticized his desire to break away and create his own path, but he was searching for something bigger and each of those previous jobs just didn't fill that desire. His search created a sense of uneasiness within him and caused him to look elsewhere. At the time, he couldn't quite define what he was looking for, but he knew he was meant for more. He shares how most people live this way, day to day without knowing what they want, no goals, little ambition and a lack of dreaming bigger.

~ Dream Bit ~
Big Dreamers Have An Inner-Knowing

Big Dreamers prefer not to follow the status quo. They have no desire to be a spectator and they work towards igniting their deeper passion at an early age. They take action. They don't allow failures to hold them back from achieving more. They look at the learning within every failure and propel themselves forward always fixating on the end goal.

Aaron grew up in the era and rising of Silicon Valley. He shares how everyone's dream was to work for one of these massive high-tech giants. Eventually, he succumbed to the societal pressures, and a friend got him a job working for a high-tech corporation. At the time, he was very proud of his achievement. He was floundering from job to job, so he felt his family would be proud of this accomplishment. However, after spending some time in this new role that familiar uneasiness surfaced once again. This was a feeling that Aaron came to recognize, like winds of change, urging him to move on and pursue the Big Dreamer inside of him.

One Monday morning, he found himself looking up from the maze of cubicles. He noticed a similar look on everyone's face as if they were plugged into a system and he didn't feel like he fit in. It reminds me of the famous Super Bowl commercial that Apple launched in 1984. You remember the one, where hundreds of bald workers are all standing in dusty ruins, listening to an Orwellian figure talking down at them? Then suddenly, a striking young female athlete wearing red shorts enters the scene, while being chased by a series of security guards. Her one mission is to free these slaves. She stops, performs three circular motions, and eventually propels a heavy sledgehammer at the massive screen; instantly shattering the Orwellian image. The workers begin to shout in unison, as they are somehow awakened from their hypnotic state.

Aaron felt as if he needed to break free from the monotony and comfort of this lifestyle that he knew would one day suppress his passion. He didn't want to be a part of this system, and with his dream machine turned on; it urged him to look up and on to the next chapter of his life. He couldn't see an end result that would truly fulfill him from being a part of this system. He witnessed some of his co-workers give over 40 years of their life to this one corporation. "How could they give this much of their energy to one corporation without some type of finish line," he asked himself? "What did they have to show for themselves and what did it all mean," he adds? These were the kinds of questions that would haunt and motivate him to look for something deeper and more connected to his dreams.

He reflects on his school system and the energy that transfused this way of existing in the world. He was a good student, but not great. He knew that his passion, extended far beyond the world of academia. While in high school, he found greater fulfillment by participating in sports. He excelled at basketball as well as track and field. These sports represented the genesis in learning the power of goal setting. "To succeed in sports, you have to know where you're going. You train for the ultimate prize, measure your results and set your mind on achieving that goal," he adds.

~ Dream Bit ~
Big Dreamers Create Big Goals

Big Dreamers are motivated by the creation of bigger goals for themselves. They imagine the feeling of crossing the threshold in their minds before it even happens in reality. They condition their mind, body and spirit on a regular basis and see themselves as winners. Big Dreamers know that every defeat is temporary and moves them closer to living their ultimate life.

By the age of 21, Aaron moved out of his parent's home and focused on fulfilling his bustling independence. He was involved in a relationship with a girlfriend that his parents disapproved of. His passion for creating a life separate from the conformity of his family intensified and this energy created a disconnection with his family and friends. He was breaking away from the system that was telling him how he should live his life and who he should be. His family and friends could not understand why he would quit his job to pursue a life as an entrepreneur. Surprisingly, the opinions of others didn't really affect Aaron or his mission as an entrepreneur. The relationship with his family and friends grew further apart and they labelled his actions and choices as unstable. Aaron didn't see it that way though, he had developed a mindset of resilience. It wasn't that he couldn't keep a job; he simply viewed the world from a different vantage point. He didn't see himself as being better, but he saw himself as a Big Dreamer and he believed in his own inner-power. He followed his intuition, in spite of feeling alone and isolated from his family and friends. He saw their way as limiting his potential. He believed his life purpose went beyond making money to only pay the bills. Aaron perceived a different reality and possibility than his friends and his siblings. "My siblings did exactly what our parents told them to do. They lived at home, attended school, focused on getting good grades and then a good job," he adds. His siblings didn't start working in their careers until the age of 30. They had already spent a third of their lives following what others told them to do and how to live. This way of existing didn't make sense to him.

Big Dreamers

Aaron laughingly shares, how he wasn't just the apple that fell off the tree, he was the apple that fell off the tree, next to a cliff! He embraced this point of differentiation from his family. He relished in blazing his own trail and with every choice and action he felt alive and on purpose with his life.

Even though Aaron was clear on what he didn't want; life as an entrepreneur was a long and arduous journey. He shares how he was not an overnight success. It's one of the reasons why some people choose the comfort of immediate satisfaction through exchanging their time for pay. Entrepreneurs look to the long-term future and they know that there are no short cuts to the success that they are creating; and they embrace the freedom of owning their own time. It was this understanding and having this energy that drove him all those years as a struggling entrepreneur. He was filled with a greater sense of meaning and purpose that made him feel alive. He relished at the idea of consciously making his own decisions and refusing not to follow the status quo. Part of what drove him was proving that this way of existing in the world was possible.

The emotional disconnect that existed between Aaron and his family propelled him forward. It became a necessary discomfort, fuelling his greatest growth.

~ Dream Bit ~

Big Dreamers Don't Follow The Status Quo

Big Dreamers look for the deeper meaning in everything and ask the answers to reveal themselves. They are not terribly fond of rules and embrace their uniqueness in the world. They look for opportunities to induce levels of discomfort for they see change as a pivotal catalyst for growth. They disrupt the system by disrupting themselves.

A big part of Aaron, wanted to prove to his family and friends that there was more to life than following what others say, you should do with your life. "In high school sports, everyone was cheering me on, but the moment I chose to break away from the corporate system, that's when the applause stopped," he recounted. This detachment from his family and friends started taking its toll on him. He considered surrendering to all the pressure and succumb to the system, just to avoid feeling so isolated. This is why most people avoid breaking away and creating their own path, they want to avoid being isolated from the rest of the world. They prefer the comfort of fitting in, versus standing out and challenging the system. There was a part of Aaron that wanted to please his family and friends. "It would have been so much simpler if I just chose to pursue an easier path," he adds. But, once again, the Big Dreamer was ignited and a booming voice encouraged him to follow his heart.

He reflects on our conversation and how feeling disconnected from the non-supporters became his greatest teachers. Without this disconnect in the earlier part of his life, he wouldn't have grown into the successful leader who is inspiring thousands of people today. Sometimes it's hard to see the light in the darkest moments of our lives, and it can be challenging to believe that God only sends us angels to guide us in becoming who we are born to be. I believe and shared with him that the isolation and disconnection he experienced for so many years was truly his greatest gift. It shaped and nourished his desire to become an independent man, free from the shackles of what our society deems as conventional. He wasn't interested in hurting anyone, nor was he attempting to create a rebellious movement, he was simply focused on blazing his own trail. This gift taught Aaron to believe in himself.

~ Dream Bit ~
Big Dreamers Believe In The Unseen

Big Dreamers recognize they live in a world governed by unique laws of attraction. They believe in the creative domain of the unconscious mind and their ability to access all of their power from it. They feel their connection to the energy of the universe and their ability to shape and define their own reality.

His years of failed attempts eventually took their toll on his relationship with his girlfriend. What started out, as a belief in his vision, eventually became a wedge in their relationship. She left him emotionally and spiritually; and Aaron once again, found himself alone and facing another crossroads in his life. His girlfriend couldn't understand how he could exist this way. Aaron was living in a tornado of emotions. Everything around him was swirling in turmoil, yet he was in the centre of the storm. There he could see the light above. In that state, he was calm and accessed his inner belief to help him stay the course. His vision for something bigger served as his compass, helping him navigate through a sea of discomfort and a lack of support from those closest to him. Big Dreamers often experience loneliness and it's through these times of deep isolation that one needs to find their inner GPS in order to move forward and stay the course. Aaron knew that the success he dreamed of for so many years would take time to manifest. He recognized that others around him wouldn't embrace his choices. There was an indescribable force at work, revealing a vision of a better future for him.

When the relationship with his girlfriend ended, he made a choice to walk away and leave everything behind. A larger gap now existed with his family and friends from the years of disconnect and it prevented him from seeking out support. He had nowhere to turn and for the first time in his life he truly felt alone. He knew if he went home his family would push him to abandon his dreams and return to his former corporate life. He feared this reality above all else, but for a moment questioned if his friends and family might be right. He shuttered at the thought of having to get back into a straight line and follow the status quo.

This part of his life truly became a defining moment. Would he choose to continue with the struggle, or return home to face embarrassment from his family and friends? He knew he could simply choose to let go of his ego and return home feeling defeated. This decision felt more like he was surrendering his dreams and his life force though. He made the choice to hang on to his dignity. He threw all of his clothes into his car and lived there for the next 6 months. His only view out onto the world was through his windshield. He didn't have anyone to turn to, until a friend in Los Angeles encouraged him to join his business.

He decided to make the drive to Los Angeles and see what his entrepreneurial friend was creating. To his bewilderment, his friend was in a worse predicament than Aaron. He quickly realized that he couldn't rely on his friends or other external resources. If Aaron were going to change his life, it would be the result of his own belief, desire and action to drive this change. What he did see in his Los Angeles friend was similar values, desires and entrepreneurial energies, which he found encouraging. He was pleased that he started attracting other Big Dreamers, who shared a common interest in wanting more out of life.

Despite this attraction to Los Angeles, Aaron was still living out of his car. "Regardless of how great people say the weather in L.A. is, when you're sleeping at night alone in your car, it's freezing cold," he recounted. These few months of living in his car, became the push he needed to get his life moving in a forward direction. He knew he needed to change his surroundings and his life. An emotional Aaron shares the difficulty in reliving this time in his life. It was at this point, where I was truly driven, to know how he overcame these challenges spiritually, emotionally and physically. These were definitely the most challenging times of Aaron's life. "The view outside my windshield was bleak and things were certainly not great for me," he adds. He spent years, struggling at creating a meaningful life. He left his family to pursue his own independence and was now living in the back seat of his car with only $40 in his pocket. He existed day-by-day, surviving on one chicken sandwich a day. Filled with tears, he shares with me that somehow he believed this would not be the end of his story. "What I knew for certain, was that I would not leave this earth dying alone in my car," shares an emotional Aaron.

He didn't have a way out, nor did he know how, but he knew he was a born as a Big Dreamer and believed in his power. Even during the lowest point in his life he believed with every cell in his body he was meant for more. Sitting in his car, glimpses of a different life filled with love, hope, possibility and greater abundance appeared in his mind. He didn't have anything but a car, a few clothes and $40 in his pocket. He didn't need anything else though, because he had his belief in something bigger that filled his heart, his stomach and his dreams. In his mind, he was not hungry, but rather filled with love and compassion. He had a spirit that was ready to soar. He felt he had wings and he knew if he just continued to set his sights higher, he could fly to the destination he imagined in his mind.

I love the premise of this chapter, "believe". It's an insight that I share in my previous book titled: *I Don't Know What the Hell I'm Doing!*® Without a deeper belief that he was meant for more, Aaron would have followed a safer and more conventional path. Without a relentless belief in his dreams, he would have chosen to remain in line and take the road less travelled.

Big Dreamers Are Driven By An Energy Of Courage

Big Dreamers fight against all odds to realize their dream. They go inward and harness a deeper energy that somehow propels them forward. Their courage and willingness to sacrifice everything inspires a new level of belief in us all. They take the road less travelled even though it sometimes creates a certain level of loneliness and isolation.

It's this energy of belief that now fuels his expanding global business. It drives him to ensure that no one in his organization ever feels alone. It's an energy that he coaches and instils within his team and in his family everyday. He never looses sight of where he came from and how his belief ignited his monumental success from the ashes of the most challenging times of his life. This is a part of his past that he doesn't offer up freely with audiences. Big Dreamers often prefer to keep this level of vulnerability, tucked away safely, in the back of their minds. I'm compelled to delve deeper into this part of Aaron's sub conscious. I believe it's this energy that truly represents the early catalyst for shaping this man's extraordinary skills as a world-class leader. It is Aaron's life journey that inspires me to share his story with the world. It's easy to look at highly successful people and not be aware of what it took them to arrive at such a place. We are baffled and we somehow assume they created instant success over night, but I think we have an opportunity to learn from their lessons and apply them to our journey.

Interestingly, I find myself drawn to movies that depict this form of reinvention. I love seeing the transformation from one state to another. I am in awe of Aaron's resolve to not give up on himself and his dreams of creating something bigger despite the odds and challenges he faced.

I can only imagine what he experienced. With the stroke of every key on my laptop I strive to capture the energy of his journey though and present it to you in a way that celebrates this man's legacy. I have visions of Aaron's grandchildren and future generations, reading this book at dinner tables and holiday gatherings. It's a legacy I'm compelled to create for these leaders I call Big Dreamers. I see the energy of this chapter and this book igniting millions of people to break away from the temporary comforts of society and become inspired to clear a new path and create their own way; and for this I am grateful for the opportunity to shine a light on Aaron and his story.

Still in his early 20's, Aaron's persistence led him to the field of telecommunications, where he started to experience a roller coaster of success. He was focused on a way up and out of the exertion. He hustled his way by talking to anyone willing to listen to his business opportunity. His journey through network marketing eventually launched him out of the car and into renting a room in a house.

For the next few years, he kept his head down and was on track to creating the first wave of his early success, and did so by outworking everybody around him. He reflects on the special gifts that his parents taught him, which were hard work, persistence and determination. His efforts and strategy of outworking everyone else eventually helped him work his way up in the ranks within his new telecommunications company. He became a top income earner and things felt great. For the first time in his life, he could see and feel his dreams taking flight. This was the reality he believed was possible and one he had shared with his family and friends for so many years.

Shortly after becoming a top income earner, his company announced that they were going to be hosting a conference. As a top income earner, he was selected as one of the keynote speakers. He was now ready to share his newfound success with his family and friends. He invited them to come out and see what he had built. This was his opportunity to enlighten and educate his parents as to the journey he'd been on these past few years. At this point, he had risen to the top of the company, but hadn't shared his success with his family. They had no idea what he was up to or the type of work he was involved in.

He had spent the past few years preparing for this special opportunity to show his parents just how hard he worked. He was their son and he wanted them to experience his success on the big stage. He wanted them to be proud of his accomplishments and witness that he had not wasted his life, but rather, created it! To Aaron's complete surprise and utter astonishment his company closed their doors a few days before the big event. The owners took off with all the money and he lost everything he worked so hard to build. His team immediately dissolved in front of his eyes. Unable to access any of the websites and databases he was re-experiencing the feelings of isolation and abandonment; and unlike before, he was falling from a much higher platform and he had a lot more to lose. Now in his late 20's, he felt angry and betrayed by the powers above. "Why God, why now and why are you doing this to me?" he would think.

This significant set back and fall from success didn't leave Aaron feeling defeated, however. It only made him dream bigger. Overcome with deep emotion during our interview, Aaron continues to relive the feeling of not giving up. He's proud of himself and I feel it in his energy, as if he was being tested by some higher power and he knew he was going to pass the test.

Despite the massive and relentless climb ahead, he started to prepare himself to create it all over again. He began his search for a new company. He shares how he was unsure of where to go at this point. He had a long-held desire to attract an inspiring role model and believed the person would soon present himself or herself. He was focused on someone he could emulate. He knew this was crucial to the next level of growth, so he started his search for someone worthy of modelling. He was no longer interested in following the pack that led him to his first success and failure. He was now ready to lead himself.

His search continued for several years, from company to company, all the while, never giving up on his dream. Instead of seeing each move as a set back, he chose to see it as a step closer to what he was seeking. He was on a journey, where everyone and everything served as his teacher. He remained open and laser focused on what he wanted in a company. He refers to this time of his life, as the dark ages. He was looking for the light at the end of the tunnel. Aaron was in a massive state of reinvention and pouring himself into company after company only to see his efforts fall short. He built his business over and over as a result of these failed companies. "When someone looks at a successful person, they don't realize the amount of effort and years of struggle they have poured themselves into," he shares. "I just wasn't prepared to give up on my dreams," he adds.

~ Dream Bit ~

Big Dreamers Fail Forward

Big Dreamers understand their journey takes years of effort by failing forward. They don't see failure as a set back, but as a means to advance their vision. With every failed attempt they create course corrections by applying the teachings to their future goals.

After years of searching, aiming and taking action on hitting his targets he was starting to lose steam. His family finally reached out to him, encouraging him to find another, more traditional way to exist. His brothers and sisters landed themselves good jobs and were finally moving out of their parent's home. His parents were now alone, so his family encouraged Aaron to consider coming back and caring for them. He saw this as a major failure and step backwards in his life. He was not ready to settle on his big dream of becoming a successful entrepreneur. Although he was crushed, he knew that he had to regroup, so he could refocus. Aaron felt that he was not defeated and saw this temporary set back, as an opportunity to regroup financially and recalibrate his vision. He had no choice, he spent the past few years continually chasing the next new start up company, building team after team, only to see them fail and his efforts go to waste. He was emotionally exhausted and financially drained at this point. So he chose to do what any good son would do. He let go of his pride and made the decision to move in and help his parents. His family was pleased and embraced his decision.

~Dream Bit ~

Big Dreamers Embrace The Ride

Big Dreamers decide what they want most. They place a strong intention on pursuing it.
This kind of energy eventually reveals the way. The line to your field goal is never a perfect
and straight one. It consists of twists and curves and backward loops.
The key is to enjoy the thrill of this roller coaster ride.

After moving home, he chose to place his entrepreneurial pursuits on the back burner. He accepted a full-time job in a previous corporation. Although it was disappointing for him, the universe was about to reveal it's extraordinary plans. It was in this twist of events, that he met the love of his life, Cathy. He knew why he was meant to be here, in this place, at this moment in time. If anyone of his past efforts had succeeded he probably never would have decided to return home, move in with his parents and accept a corporate job. The universe was masterfully opening his heart to receive the love he never knew he was capable of receiving. He was a driven man, filled with passion and pride, but he knew he deserved to receive love and God decided to send him one of his most special angels, Cathy.

As he spent more time with her, he shared his incredible journey and vision. He revealed all of his past ambitions, goals, set backs and failures. It was as if he was a pirate in search of some lost treasure. Cathy sat and listened attentively with wonderment. She witnessed the great passion in his heart. His eyes would light up when he shared his bigger dreams and the life he imagined creating. He poured his heart out to Cathy and shared all of his temporary successes, as well as his multitude of failed attempts. It was as if he needed someone to witness his life and feel his heart after being isolated for so many years. An incredible feeling of joy washed over him the more he opened up and shared his dreams and aspirations with her. He had a new purpose for coming to work. He would leap out of bed every morning at the thought of seeing Cathy and sharing more of his journey with her. He was compelled to share his dreams, as if she had a magic carpet, and would one day carry them off into the sunset together.

Choosing to return home now seemed to take on a different meaning. It wasn't just about caring for his aging parents it was about his time with Cathy. This intersection seemed to ignite a powerful force inside of him. Even though he was filled with gratitude to be employed, it also felt like an anchor holding him down on the ocean floor. He felt like a ship docked in port waiting for his opportunity to sail away onto his next adventure. A restless desire was now burning inside of him. He knew he was meant for more. Visions of his dream life flashed faster and more furiously. He was alive with the possibility of igniting what he originally started. Would Cathy join him though? The thought that she might would fill him with tremendous joy. Perhaps, that is what he was lacking all these years. Perhaps it was the love he was seeking that would help bridge the gap and accelerate his success. He had an inner knowing that he was destined for success. His life was an exalted mission of profound change and impact. No matter where he worked or what he pursued this energy of change was always present. It continually flowed through him and he remained open to new opportunities.

He knew he would be ok to leave everything behind and continue on with his dream. Even though he was on the fast track to corporate success this was not the ladder he desired to climb. Most people would have given up on this hopeless pursuit and struggle that he endured for so many years, but Aaron knew he had only one life to live, and he was a crusader on a mission. Visions of receiving a gold watch after 25 years of existing in this corporate culture haunted him. He was prepared to start at ground zero with nothing but a vision and a dream to fuel his own success. He faced his fears, and once again, let the current of his inner knowing lead him to his next journey.

He continued to share with Cathy his ambitions and desire to give the corporation his two-weeks notice. Her energy and belief in him became a firework in his soul. All those months of conversations, ignited his dream and encouraged him to aim high and fly. He was ready to shoot for the moon. Nothing would hold him back. These past 12 months, felt like rocket fuel and a new source of energy was propelling him forward. Every interaction with Cathy intensified his focus and strengthened his resolve. He was mentally and emotionally prepared to leave his comfort zone and venture forward, once again, into the unknown. He felt like an old-world explorer, venturing into the open sea, with his passion and desire serving as his north star. Cathy was the wind in his sails.

However, things at home were good. His family finally approved his lifestyle. They loved the conservative approach he had taken these past 12 months. He embraced a corporate role with a stable income and found a new girlfriend whom they highly approved of for him. In their minds, he was finally in alignment with the path of his siblings.

~ Dream Bit ~
Big Dreamers Collaborate

Big Dreamers don't do it alone. They form collaborations with others. They surround themselves with people that believe and support their vision. They continually take action and lean into their dreams. They attract like-minded people to join their tribe.

Throughout this time back home, Aaron still managed to stay actively in touch with friends in Los Angeles, who were starting up another new business. They continually urged him to come back and join them, but he was torn. He knew he had to make a change, but what was that change and was it the right timing? Yet again, he arrived at a crossroads. His parents were finally proud of him and he was living a normal and structured life. He had found employment with a reputable corporation with promotional opportunities and had found this new and amazing relationship. Was moving back to Los Angeles and pursuing the life of a struggling entrepreneur the right choice? He thought, "How would it be different and how could I leave everything behind?"

After much deliberation, Aaron did the only thing he knew would fulfill him. He lavished at the idea of pursuing his journey as an entrepreneur. This did not make his family happy and it wasn't a decision they supported. Quite the contrary, they were baffled and belittled his decision. They did whatever they could to talk some real sense into him. "I lost whatever credibility I had managed to create with my parents during those past 12 months," he adds. In their minds, he was delusional and in need of a serious family intervention! "How many more times do you want to fail Aaron? You have tried this before so many times. Why should now be any different?" they would say. He knew there was something big waiting for him on the horizon though. He could see and feel success. He was optimistic and recognized that this was his time, and was he ever right! Shortly after joining his friends in L.A., his patience and persistence paid off. He managed to make his way to the top of the company fairly quickly and held a successful role with this company for a few years.

With his newfound success, together with Cathy, he eventually chose to leave and join up with a science-based supplement company. Aaron and Cathy were impressed with the quality of the product and through months of hard work and commitment they accelerated to the top ranks and became million dollar earners within the first few years. He shares how diligently they worked and how their efforts blew away the owners of the company. He was one of the most successful leaders and together with Cathy they blazed a major trail and expanded globally. In a few short years, he even surpassed his original up line-sponsor and was now reaping the benefits of living as a top income earner. His family still did not understand what he was doing or how he was earning this kind of substantial income. "My family thought I was some sort of door-to-door salesmen pushing healthy vitamins onto people," he shares. "They didn't embrace life as an entrepreneur and they criticized my choices," he adds. He was continually compared to his siblings. His sister became a nurse who married a police officer. His brother became an engineer who married an accountant. Aaron's entire family had built their livelihood through more traditional means. He was always proud of his siblings, but he simply chose to pursue a path that was unique to him. His parents, sadly, labelled his behaviour as unstable. They pleaded with him to give up on his foolish pursuits and once again, embrace a more conservative path like that of his siblings.

For years, he viewed himself as a failure in the eyes of his parents, whom he respected tremendously. He continually felt the pressure to release his dreams in pursuit of a safer and more traditional existence. These were some of the challenges he faced at every crossroads. He possessed a desire to win the respect and admiration of his parents, and this energy seemed to drive him even harder.

Even after experiencing success, he believed his parents would never embrace his path. He respected his family, however, he was tired of being perceived as a rebel, while his siblings were praised for following traditional and more conservative paths. "A traditional lifestyle, just wasn't my way or the future I envisioned for myself," he adds. He was strong-willed and chose to create an independent life for himself. He lavished at the idea not feeding off of his hard-working parents. He chose a non-traditional route and challenged the status quo in order to create his success.

Aaron had spent months living and sleeping out of his car, with little cash in his pocket. He swallowed his pride to return home, broken and penniless to care for his aging parents. Aaron is the epitome of a Big Dreamer. He is a man who never gave up on his pursuit for living as a Big Dreamer. He could have succumb to the pressures of society and family by living at home and being comfortable in his corporate job. He could have given into his own fears and doubts, after experiencing a myriad of failed attempts; and taken the easy and traditional path. However, much of his success is a result of his relentless belief in the unseen and in himself. He defied the odds by never giving up. "My relatives often expressed that I was the bad apple," he recounted. Hearing the rejection and disbelief from his family brought him to tears, more than one time. "These words were like sharp-pointed spears, that seem to penetrate my heart," he shares

~Dream Bit ~
Big Dreamers Are Highly Resilient

Big Dreamers care very little of what others think. They don't allocate or waste precious energy worrying what others might say. They condition themselves by blocking out the noise. They don't allow the disbelief from others to influence their greater purpose.

I asked Aaron if his parents ever came around and acknowledged his success? He laughed and shared how they eventually did. It took a considerable amount of years though and it was only after he and Cathy had reached the Million Dollar Club status. Despite all the challenges and negative energy he experienced with his family, he was still able to rise above it all. He put his feelings and ego aside and chose to help retire his 75-year-old parents who were still working at the time. From all of his accomplishments, helping to retire his parents represents the greatest milestone for him. "I knew they would never retire, unless I was going to help them do it," he recounts. He couldn't help but think and compare that no matter how much he could have earned at a full-time corporate job, it would have never been enough to fulfill this meaningful goal, so that his parents could live out the rest of their life with peace. It was this energy that fuelled his bigger dreams and what compelled him to become a successful entrepreneur. His parents resisted his ambitious pursuit as an entrepreneur, and ironically it was this persistence and belief that his parents now benefit from everyday. He enthusiastically shares how the energy shifted upon retiring his parents. "My parents finally told me, that my siblings should have joined me," he laughs. No matter the challenges he faced in rebuilding his businesses numerous times over, none of that affected him as much as his mom's disbelief and constant comparison to his siblings. "My mom has a selective memory! Every time she sees me, she tells me how she was always my biggest cheerleader," he adds.

He finally arrived and became what he was seeking. He and his wife Cathy had become one of the three top income earners in their supplement company. His daily actions were continually fuelled by his passion for serving others. He truly exists to support and lead his team. When he finally secured a leadership role in the company, he began to uncover some disturbing realizations about the ownership. He appealed to the owners to create a stronger infrastructure that would help his team experience greater levels of success in far less time. He soon realized though that his appeals and intentions fell on deaf ears. This growing lack of support, from the ownership raised a series of red flags and it conflicted with his deeper purpose to serve others. Aaron and Cathy were attracted to the deeper values instilled by the original owner. Like most large companies, these original values can often become lost with new generations of ownership. He was a loyal leader and follower, and as one of the top income earners he had a deep desire to collaborate more effectively with the owners. He knew that together they could help thousands of people reach new levels of success in shorter time frames. Sadly, the new CEO, which was the original owners son wasn't interested in implementing any of Aaron's ideas.

He found himself at a crossroads once again. He had a strong feeling that his long-term goals of helping thousands of people enrich their lives did not align with the ownership of this company anymore. He loved the industry, yet he recognized, something had to change. He predicted that the owners wouldn't change their mindset, so he chose to change himself, and ultimately, seek out a new company to partner with.

153

Things were far more different for Aaron and Cathy at this stage of their lives. They had the financial means to retire, yet he still had a burning desire to help thousands of people create the same success he and Cathy created. He existed to be and do something special with his life. He had a long-held desire to inspire and help others achieve greater levels of freedom. However, his values and beliefs, that he held so dear to his heart, no longer aligned with this company. He found himself questioning his own personal ethics. He felt compromised and didn't want his name attached to this brand. "How could I let them use me as their poster child, when I don't believe in how they're building their company, on the backs of innocent people," he recounted.

After weeks of deep contemplation, he shared with Cathy, how he could no longer help build this company. Everyday he remained associated with this company the more they challenged his beliefs. He encouraged Cathy to leave the company and rebuild somewhere that shared their vision. He was prepared to leave it all and build a new legacy. "I finally understood, why so many of these companies had failed. It was the result of them not having a soul. This was the energy that was always missing in everyone of these companies that I invested my time in building," he recounted. He recognized what he was looking for in a partner and he believed that the right company and the right opportunity would present itself.

~ Dream Bit ~
Big Dreamers Serve Others With Their Purpose

Big Dreamers experience fulfillment by serving others. Their driving Why is deeply rooted in creating greater meaningful outcomes in the lives of others. They embrace change and discomfort for they clearly know it leads to their growth.

Aaron was confident in who he was and what he stood for. He was all about serving people and he knew what fuelled his greater purpose. It was this clear connection to his deeper driving Why that attracted him a new company, which shared his deeper values. "To be a successful entrepreneur you have to find a way to bring tremendous value to people, through service to others", he adds.

I asked him to reflect on the teachings and lessons of his life. I asked him to share what he would say to the younger, homeless Aaron, who had to sleep in his car? "I would encourage my younger self to stay strong, stick to what I believe in, and know that I am destined for a life of greatness," he shares. His journey reveals, that life is going to hit you with a lot of challenges that are beyond your control and you will fall many times. He shares a profound message of courage and legacy though, when he says, "it's your story and it's going to stop when you say it's over." He later noted, "you have to keep riding and you have to keep moving forward." Everything in life that is thrust upon us is a test from the universe, questioning us as to how bad we really want it. "I would tell my younger self, to ensure I pass all those tests," he adds.

The deeper shift in his life was always present at every crossroads. This energy instilled a deeper knowing that his story would not end during those challenging times, when it would have been easier to give in. He innately knew if he just kept pushing himself, he would eventually emerge a new and successful man. As he shares these deeper reflections with me, he pauses, his eyes filling up with tears as if recalling a memory of his younger self, actually coming into contact with the much older and wiser Aaron.

I am inspired with this deep and reflective conversation. I'm filled with gratitude to be a part of this extraordinary man's life and his gift in taking me along his epic journey. He is a Big Dreamer, who never gave up, even when faced with tremendous odds. He was alone, cold and hungry for so many years. He felt lost, abandoned and disconnected from his family. His hunger went far beyond just food. He craved to change the course of his life and the lives around him. He felt at a deeper level he could change his life and his parents. He has embraced the energy that was always present throughout his life. He transformed himself and he clearly interprets the power of synchronicity. He lives his life with a belief that greatness, flows within all of us. It's the willingness to push beyond the pain and leap over the hurdles that helps us manifest our greatest desires. Losing everything, feeling a sense of abandonment and starting over, numerous times shaped him into the man he is today. He is a servant and passionate leader, whom exist to serve others.

Looking back on his epic journey, he carries with him a deep sense of pride in his ability to look up and find light in the darkest hours. It was as if his older self somehow defied time by extending a hand and pulling him upward. There existed an energy that always kept him focused on looking beyond the windshield to a promising future ahead. Even during the most trying times he never played small. He persevered without cheers, medals or praise from his family. He never let his current reality become his only reality. He believed he was a Big Dreamer with the ability to create and define his life. He believed in his vision and knew if he just stayed the course he could manifest anything he set his mind to. He lived in the moment, but was defined by his future self, one that he saw clearly and served him as the ultimate GPS.

Aaron defied the status quo and his earlier childhood programming which taught him to conform and fit in. He shares how it's this need for external validation and acceptance from others that holds us back from truly growing into a bigger version of ourselves.

The beliefs bestowed on him from his parents never managed to latch onto his neural programming. He challenged it at every turn without fear or judgment from others. "The world consists of people dressing and acting the way they think the world wants them to look and act, but in actual fact they are just conforming in order to fit in," he adds. He shares how so many people allow the perceptions of others to hold them back from dreaming bigger. "It's as if people allow others to define the ceiling of what we're capable of reaching," he shares. There are NO LIMITS to what your mind is capable of creating. I love the football analogy that he shares with me - a quarterback struggling to hold onto the football is like us struggling to hold onto our dreams. "As the quarterback runs down the field with his dream tucked tightly into his body he sees the end zone, yet the other players continually try and steal the football from him. He has to protect his dream from the other players that want to take it away from him", and so do we!

Aaron's Top Actions for Dreaming Bigger:

Aaron's definition of success is freedom, which he defines as, "the break away from how society would have you live." With great success you are able to inspire others to be the best version of themselves. With every step forward he experienced greater levels of belief in himself and in the way he was creating it. "Every action strengthens your core belief," he adds.

- You need to believe in your dream
- You need to protect your dream from the dream killers.

- You need to fill yourself up first before giving to others. Aaron was always a big giver, but he had to learn how to fill up his cup of tea first.

- Instead of just giving to others focus your efforts on inspiring them.

- Help others develop the capacity to look up and nurture their own inner-strength. As he was moving up higher in levels, he was able to see more clearly. He never stopped shining a light on others, and helped them create a clearer picture of their desired life. He epitomizes next level leadership by applying his knowledge and wisdom towards advancing others.

- As an entrepreneur, your number one goal is to inspire others by leading from the front through self-sacrifice. "You have to be prepared to do what others are not prepared to do, but to inspire them along the way," he adds. This is the one consistent goal that carried him to the top of the heap.

Aaron embraced a new mindset in building his global business with Cathy. In his earlier companies, he would obtrude his vision for the success on others. He now embraces the need to allow others to fail and create their own journey. He lives with a greater sense of flow through the energy of others, by helping them define their own way. He encourages others through inspiration rather than control. "I realize that by allowing others to find their own way the person they desire to become will emerge throughout their journey to success," he adds.

~ Dream Bit ~
Big Dreamers Inspire Others

Big Dreamers inspire others by getting out of their way. They don't impose their ideals on others. They believe dreams are temporary and remain open. They realize dreams are stepping-stones in a much greater creation. They continually develop themselves, so they can have a more profound impact on everyone around them.

He achieved great levels of success in all areas of his life. He is now focused on nurturing his greater purpose. As he continues on with this next chapter of his extraordinary life, he is becoming a shimmering haven for others through greater levels of inspiration. He has a long-held desire to contribute to other people's lives, and be a role model to his beautiful daughter. He is living his legacy now in the greatest time of his life. Contrasted to the younger, driven Aaron, he now seeks greater peace, love and harmony. It's these valuable life lessons that give greater meaning to his existence. He relishes in all of the details of his life. Sitting on the beach and listening to the waves crashing up on the shore, he basks in the love of seeing his daughter run towards him with open arms. He has arrived, yet he celebrates the journey of his life by inspiring others to live their legacy. "When I was smart, I wanted to change the world, but now that I'm wiser, I want to change myself," he shares. "By being an example and living a life of giving, sharing and inspiring, I know that my daughter will embrace those values" he adds. His greatest wish for you is to know that you can exist and live your greatest life now. You can live as a Big Dreamer by casting away your limiting beliefs that no longer serve you. You can chose to block out the influences and perceptions from others.

Aaron will be remembered as a giver and a Big Dreamer who existed to help others live their legacy. He believes in himself and lives everyday with tremendous gratitude for the life he's created. He is a loving father, husband and leader.

~ A Dedication to my Husband by Cathy Ngo ~

"You are my rock, my strength, my inspiration and my love. I always knew there was something special inside of you, Aaron. I knew from the moment I met you, that you would change the world. I never doubted you for one minute. You have always been a dreamer and you sold me on your dream life the moment you shared it with me, so many years ago. You made our life real. I don't say it often enough, but you are my strength and I have always seen and believed in you. I want you to always know how proud I am of you and how you have touched all of our lives and the lives of so many other people in the most profound way. You are forever loved."

Your love, Cathy

6. Darin Kidd
SIMPLIFY

*"I am an ever growing Christian, that serves God with all my heart
and I exist to help people become the best version of themselves."*
~ *Darin Kidd*

Darin Kidd grew up in Lynchburg, Virginia with humble surroundings. He had great parents, who raised him well, but they always seemed to struggle with finances and the topic of conversation at the dinner table seemed to revolve around how the bills would get paid. He didn't have the luxury of spending a lot of quality time with his parents since they were so consumed with working endless hours. He witnessed the struggle and challenges that his parents faced with being business owners. Life was a daily grind and struggle for the Kidd household. They spent considerable time trying to collect on unpaid client accounts.

These earlier times created a lot of anxiety and unease within Darin. "My dad couldn't afford a decent car. He made his own form of a seatbelt with foam and bean bags in the back of his pick up truck, and most of my clothes were hand me downs from neighbours," he shares. He loved and admired his parents; and speaks so highly of their work ethic. He shares with me the regret of seeing his father pass away 6 years ago without fulfilling his dreams. "My dad always lived with the energy of someday we'll do this, and someday we'll go see that, but that someday for my dad never came," he shares. This energy impacted and shaped the person that Darin is today. He prioritizes his life by placing time and experiences with his family above all else.

As a young boy, Darrin was very angry and struggled with bullying. His high school years were some of his most challenging times. He continually defended himself and even broke both of his hands fighting. Aside from having great and hard working parents, he lacked positive role models in his life. He was continually told what he was doing wrong and this energy contributed to his lack of willingness to try harder. His days were filled with worry and higher levels of anxiety as he struggled to deal with OCD. He didn't perform well in school as a result of his inability to focus and concentrate. He was bored, and often struggled to stay awake in class. Listening to others was a real challenge and even though he could hear what his teachers were saying, he struggled to apply these lessons; failing many of his tests as a result.

Throughout high school his stress factor was off the charts. He was continually stressed with having to deal with his home life, neighbourhood bullies, and his poor performance in school. His concerns with a lack of money seemed to intensify throughout high school. No matter what direction he took during his high school years, his life was in a steady decline with every daily action taking its toll. He barely made it through high school and passed by the skin

Big Dreamers

of his teeth. He knew something had to change if he was going to survive these tough and stressful teen years. It was this energy that eventually led him to explore the world of martial arts to help deal with his angry attitude.

Following high school he found himself going from job to job, and no matter how hard he tried, he just couldn't seem to retain any kind of employment. He married young and chose to drop out of college. He strained to find an anchor and foothold in life. This struggle carried on in throughout his early 20's, eventually, causing him to declare bankruptcy. Darin had his car repossessed and was forced to live on government assistance. His family was surviving off food stamps. He struggled to survive and provide for his wife and kids. He reached the lowest point in his life. He was depressed and felt as if he had let everyone around him down. No matter how hard he tried, he just couldn't seem to surface from this overwhelming abyss.

These seemed like hopeless times and he didn't know where to turn. He was lost and close to having his home taken away. "My life seemed like an avalanche of bad decisions, one after another, and my future didn't look bright," he recounted. "I found myself looking into the mirror one night and feeling completely defeated," he adds. Even in his darkest days though, Darin believed, there was a Big Dreamer living inside of him.

Big Dreamers Believe They Are Meant for More

Big Dreamers see their struggle as a catalyst for action. They don't let the outcomes of their past actions define the bigger reason for their existence. They are not defined by their past, but rather learn how to master the power of the moment. They arrive at a realization that the change they seek resides within them.

It was this belief that brought a ray of light and sparked the attraction of a series of mentors that would change the course of his life. He finally arrived at the point where he was sick and tired of being sick and tired!

Darin shared with me the fable of the farmer sitting on his front porch rocking chair. Someone visiting the farmer tells him that his dog is lying on top of a nail and the farmer responds, "Oh don't worry about it, when it gets bad enough he'll move!" Well for Darin he was now ready to pick himself up and get off that nail. "Up to this point in my life it just didn't seem to hurt bad enough," he reflects. He was no longer comfortable with existing in a sick, tired and broken state of mind.

For things to change, he knew he had to be the one to first change. Creating and providing a better future for his family drove him to this change. "Success is buried right underneath frustration, so I must have been getting close," he laughs. He had certainly reached his tipping point and was ready to start dreaming bigger. He was open to implanting a new set of positive thoughts and a new belief system into his mind. "It was at that point where I decided to post a

3" x 4" index card on my wall that simply read, 'I will until'," he adds.

In reflection, he was unable to truly see the light during those darker times. He had an optimistic outlook, however, he couldn't see these challenges as serving his greater good. He was in survival mode, so little did he know his challenge would become his greatest catalyst for growth. Today, he understands why he was meant to experience this form of anguish and he shares these lessons with thousands of people that find themselves in similar situations. He attributes much of his success due to his earlier misfortunes. "It's not the easy times that make us grow, it's the challenging ones. I chose to be better and use my adversity as a building block," he recounted. "You either go through it or grow through it," he adds.

167

The lowest point in his life was going through his daughter's plastic piggy bank in order to put food on the table. For months, they had been saving all of their spare change for a trip to Disney Land, which he had promised his younger daughter. You can imagine her devastation while witnessing her parents on the floor, sorting the change for their Disney trip fund. "We were constantly threatened by debt collectors, but nothing compares to the heartache of looking up at my daughter and seeing her eyes fill up with tears," he shares. This image of his daughter running out of the room, sobbing with tears is forever imprinted in his mind. This represents his "day of disgust." He thought "God, how could I let this happen, how could my life reach this low point?" It was this experience that drove him to dream even bigger everyday.

Every time he would find himself wanting to quit or give up on his dreams all he needed to do was close his eyes and replay this experience over and over in his mind. "When I place an emotional attachment to the success I'm pursuing, I can manifest what I desire most," he shares. And, there was certainly no shortage of these kinds of emotional images! He had many to choose from, yet nothing was more powerful to his reinvention as a Big Dreamer than the piggy bank incident. Within months, he started to experience change, through this emotional and transformational process. He began to master the art of influencing his unconscious mind with the use of powerful triggers.

~ Dream Bit ~
Big Dreamers Influence Their Mind

Big Dreamers influence the unconscious part of their mind with new and powerful thought processes. Through a collective process of daily visualization, affirmations and often meditation, Big Dreamers recondition their minds by creating new thoughts, patterns and habits. Over 97% of our untapped and unrealized power exists in this unconscious part of our minds. Big Dreamers tap into this power.

For Darin, it was a new day. His "someday" had arrived, and he was determined to seek out the knowledge that would help transform his life. What did he have to loose through gathering and applying this new knowledge? The habits he had acquired up to this point were not serving him well. The choices he had made consciously or unconsciously were not elevating his life to new levels. For things to change, he knew he had to change his thoughts, beliefs and behaviours. He had a desire to replace his bad habits with successful ones, in order to change the course of his family's future.

He began asking and living the big questions like, "Where can I get the information that I'm seeking?" Darin had a grandmother who was trained in sales for an insurance company, and one day he decided to visit her. When he shared his desire to create a significant change in his life, she presented him with an assemblage of personal development audiocassettes. One of the first tapes was by author and global speaker, Brian Tracey called, *The Psychology of Achievement.* For the next several months, he immersed himself into these audio programs using his portable cassette player.

Leading up to this point, he was unaware of the impact that reading, listening and positive associations could have on his life. "Your associations are everything and they act like an elevator, either taking your life up or down," he shares. "Listening to these audio tapes everyday had such a profound impact on me," he recounted. A message and emphasis of positive association was being drilled deeper into his subconscious mind.

From there, he focused on changing the course of his future. He no longer viewed his past as his only reality. He felt he had a way forward and upward. He had a long-held desire to attract business mentors he felt he lacked in his life. Up to this point all he had were the voices from his personal development audio books, but he lavished at the thought of seeing and experiencing these mentors at live seminars. At the time, he was unable to afford an admission ticket to these kinds of events, but it didn't stop him from dreaming of sitting in the front row and meeting his future mentors.

He was starving for more audio programs. He was burning through batteries to power his portable cassette player, and was determined to soak in as much personal development as possible. His cassette player served as his direct link to the mentors and it filled his mind with the possibility for a better life. He knew he had to saturate his mind with positive messages in order to reprogram it. His ears were literally on fire and he was thirsty for more high-level inspiration. The messages started sinking in and he found himself retaining the information contained within these audio programs, despite the earlier learning challenges he experienced in high school. He could feel a change expanding within him. He had found a way to ignite his dream machine again. His philosophy and attitude once filled with anger and anxiety, was now replaced with hope and inspiration. "It took a lot of work and persistence for me to replace a life time of conditioned stink'n-think'n," he recounts.

Struggling to provide for his growing family, he found himself moving from job to job; listening to his audio mentors every chance he had. After years of hard work, he eventually landed a corporate sales position in the gift and sales industry. He successfully managed to achieve the highest grossing sales across the entire South East territory of the United States. "The funny thing is, I had struggled at matching socks with a suit, but here I am with a sales responsibility of aesthetically dressing up gift shops," he laughs. "To paraphrase Jim Rohn, I had to make up in numbers what I lacked in skill," he adds. He attributes his sales success to his ability to outwork his colleagues. However, despite all his success and hard work, his company ended up cutting his territory in half and Darin was once again looking for work.

He continued on his journey, volunteering on the weekends and moving from job to job, continually experiencing layoffs when the companies were sold. He believed his life was meant for more. He was no longer satisfied with just scraping by and was prepared to put his recent knowledge of personal development to hard work. He wasn't interested in using his energy to build someone else's dream. He had enough of that! He had poured himself into traditional type jobs and he was tired of selling his time for little rewards.

He made the choice to increase his level and commitment to personal development. He was determined to attract the right mentors and better opportunities to build a thriving future for himself and his family. With persistence, he eventually attracted the mentors and the opportunity, but he still had to put in the time and the hard work to make it a success. "If it sounds easy, then it's sleazy. We don't make what we want, rather, we make what we are," he shares. "In order to earn more, I had to be willing to become more," he adds.

~ Dream Bit ~
Big Dreamers Are Big Readers

Big Dreamers work harder on themselves than on their business. They are big readers and are focused on continual learning. They have a strong attraction to personal development and continually seek out new and innovative ways to improve their minds.

I love the analogy of lottery winners that Darin shares with me. He explains their inability to maintain their short-term windfall and says that over 90% of lottery winners typically lose all of their winnings after the first year. They end up being in worse shape than when they first won the money. The reason for their downfall stems from their inability to develop a conscious mind and be aware of the money in order to sustain their new way of existence. Our brains are hardwired to revert to our comfort zones. "Lottery winners will do whatever they can to return to their conditioned level of income," shares Darin. They will spend their winnings and eventually take themselves back to their original comfort zone. Many lottery winners face tremendous emotional trauma, as a result of being unequipped to deal with the pressure of creating a new money mindset.

This wasn't going to be the case for Darin, he was now prepared to journey ahead and create a new wealth mindset. He was a Big Dreamer and imagined a lifestyle of more time and money. He desired to live his life to the fullest. "I knew that to grow my income, I had to first grow a new and powerful mindset," he recounted.

He continued on with his personal development journey through sheer determination. He wouldn't allow himself to become distracted by the naysayers. He could taste success and began acting as if the success had already occurred, a powerful success habit that many Big Dreamers employ. "Psychologists have proven it's far easier to act your way into a feeling than feel your way into acting, so it's important to act the way you want to feel and soon you will feel the way you act," he shares.

~ Dream Bit ~
Big Dreamers Imagine It

Big Dreamers imagine and feel their way into success. Through daily and conscious effort they visualize the feeling of actually having achieved the success they desire. They drive new levels of success through powerful intention, visualized thought and inspired actions.

"As Ralf Waldo Emerson noted, 'motion creates emotion'. Do the thing and you'll have the power," shares Darin. Even to this present day Darin doesn't wait for the right emotions to appear. There are many times when he wakes up and finds it challenging to motivate himself. "It doesn't just happen naturally," he adds. However, he began mastering the only thing he could influence and change, which was his own ability to laser focus his thoughts and get himself into powerful action. He absorbed the content from his personal development tapes and knew he could drive his success forward. He had the power to dream bigger and change the circumstances for his family. He took 100% responsibility for the new results he desired to experience in his life.

It was his goal setting, with a combination of high payoff activities that helped advance his success. "I ask myself, what are the 20% activities that will yield 80% of the results that I'm looking for in my life," he shares. Everyday he motivated himself by focusing on identifying and living high payoff activities. This new success habit eventually became a conditioned behaviour. Even when he didn't feel like it he persistently pushed himself to drive his actions forward. He turned off the noise and replaced negative self-talk with positivity.

We all have the power to create our day in advance, if we carve out the time to create new and powerful behaviours. Darin made the conscious effort to carry around his portable cassette player and flood his mind with positive thoughts that reinforced and reconditioned his mind. His mind reconditioning didn't happen overnight though. It took years of consistent and persistent effort. He took daily actions at improving and strengthening his mind. He used positive affirmations to displace older negative thinking.

~ Dream Bit ~
Big Dreamers Affirm Their Success

Big Dreamers shout out their affirmations. An affirmation is a powerful statement that starts with the words: "*I am...*" When combined with a powerful emotion, an affirmation is like a high-speed train right into your unconscious mind, where all of your power exists.

In his earlier years, he didn't understand the power of employing new success habits, yet he developed each one of them, through persistence, trust and faith. He didn't need to know what the hell he was doing, he just believed in the action of doing it consistently and persistently. "To change my life, I knew I had to tell my brain what I wanted," he adds. He worked around the clock, feeding his mind with positive thoughts of change.

~ Dream Bit ~
Big Dreamers Make Better Choices

As human beings, we make around 60,000 choices per day. Over 97% of those choices, are made in the subconscious mind. Big Dreamers fuel and influence their subconscious with the right thoughts in order to influence their behaviours.

"One of my top billionaire mentors, Paul J. Meyer, mentored me for a decade. He says, 'we magnetize the conditions we seek'. What we think about we bring about and what we focus on grows," he shares. It took Darin over a decade to truly grasp the Why behind these powerful actions that he was acting on through faith. Today, he has greater clarity behind his actions. In the past, he instinctively blocked out negative thoughts by driving positive thinking into his subconscious. He knew that one negative comment has more destructive power than a positive thought. He could no longer allow negative thoughts to dominate his life and influence his actions. "I focused on blocking the negative, that's everywhere around us and fuelled my mind with positivity, because that was what I could control," he shares.

He knew the enemy holding himself back from achieving greater success was himself. He was the lid that sealed in his potential and prevented him from becoming more. It took him a while to arrive at a deeper realization, that reaching every new level in his life was only the result of developing new and powerful belief systems. It's one of the top success principles he shares with his audiences today. He cultivated a new belief system through his positive associations and through personal development. His willingness, desire and determination to change his mind, ultimately, propelled his life forward.

Even after years of working on his mind, he still found himself struggling to really move forward. It is only in the past few years, that Darin's life truly changed, as a result of believing he was meant for more. He believed he would become the average of the five people he associated most with, and continually observed what his current associations were doing to him. If they weren't contributing to his success he knew he had to make changes. He only surrounds himself with people that believe in him. "I would rather be the one making the lowest income, in my power circle, knowing that these associations, will only help me achieve more," he shares.

He continually seeks out, attracts and surrounds himself, with visionary type thinkers that work hard and focus on building their future. He still feels the people in his life believe more in him than he does himself. "I am a continual work in progress," he shares. "It's their belief, that inspires me to be, do and achieve more," he adds.

He is filled with gratitude for the positive associations and mentors in his life. He attributes his success and ability to Dream Bigger as a result of the energy he's cultivated. He doesn't take his relationships for granted and strives to nurture them on a consistent basis. He made a conscious choice to no longer be influenced by his broke friends who were used to blaming their external circumstances for their lot in life. "Most people blame the economy and the government for their lack of success and choose to remain a victim," he shares. He has no interest in surrounding himself with that kind of negative energy and belief system. "In contrast, my wealthier friends are filled with optimism during tougher economic downturns," he adds. Big Dreamers understand the majority of wealth is made during challenging and economic slumps. This is the kind of progressive thinking that he was interested in surrounding himself with.

Eventually, he was able to see the results of his hard work paying off. He was making enough money to survive through odd jobs here and there. During his transformative years he was able to release the energy of the past that held him back. He did whatever he needed to do to survive in the present and fixated on a future he believed he could create. It took him years to break free and unseal the lid that trapped his greater potential. He spent over a decade working harder than ever, but with time was able to break $100,000 of annual income.

The reason most people can't break out of their mould stems from allowing their friends and their negative associations to hold them down. "Friends that are broke, often want to pull you back into their reality, so you won't leave them behind," he shares. "It's when I started rising up and focusing on changing my life, that's when my friends started taking swings at me," he adds. Many of these so-called friends haven't done the work on themselves and they will do anything to bring you back down to their level. His friends consistently tried to remind him of where he came from and the poverty he experienced. "It's easier for others to tear you down versus helping you build your dream," he adds.

He was no longer interested in surrounding himself with that kind of self-defeating noise. "Most people aren't willing to do what I was willing to do in order to dream bigger," he shares. It's this inward thinking that holds most people back. "Unsuccessful people, are just not willing to do what successful people do on a daily basis," he adds.

Big Dreamers

Big Dreamers Block Out The Noise

Big Dreamers shield negative energy and block out the noise from the external world. They avoid watching news or being influenced by the media. They are protective of their energy and selective in whom they choose to surround themselves with.

There were many times when he felt like quitting. Every time he felt a wave of discouragement taking its hold on him, he would flow his energy to powerful activities he believed would impact his future. It wasn't so much an inner knowing, but rather a stronger internal desire to become a different man with a different future. The more he connected with the amazing people in his life, the stronger his belief in himself grew. Darin's dream machine intensified the more he exposed himself to great mentors and personal development materials. He had an optimistic outlook for his future and was inspired with a desire to reinvent himself.

~ Dream Bit ~

Big Dreamers Think Externally

Big Dreamers are external thinkers. Their inspired actions go way beyond their current selves. They are inspired to impact many and driven by a deeper purpose. They have a desire to make a global impact and believe in their abilities to influence others with their passion and purpose.

I asked Darin to imagine himself travelling back in time and meeting up with his younger more troubled self. I was curious what life lesson he would share. "I would tell myself to be careful with whom I hung around and pick associations that would enhance my future self," he shares. "I would encourage my younger self to fuel my mind with the most positive materials," he adds.

His commitment to these two pivotal areas later on in his life influenced tremendous change in his philosophy, what he valued and how he perceived the world. These actions drove his behaviour, which ultimately influenced the outcomes in his life. His strong will and drive for change ignited a new belief within. This once shy kid, petrified of speaking in front of small groups, now finds himself confidently inspiring and training huge audiences. These past limiting beliefs that include a lack of education and professional designations no longer restrict him from standing out and impacting others.

He practices a daily approach to driving his success upward that he believes anyone can do if they choose to do so. Everyday he conditions himself by reading 10 pages of an inspiring book and listening to powerful audio programs. He transcends his powerful success habits onto his children while driving. He wants to instil these values by helping them create a powerful mind at a young age. He practices and shares what he preaches on a consistent and daily basis. He has his kids listening to 15-25 minutes of an inspiring sermon or messages by people like, Rick Warren. He then creates the space with his kids to discuss what they just listened to. He's confident this daily ritual is influencing and shaping their attitude, personal philosophy and ultimately their behaviour. He's filled with tremendous pride and gratitude for his children. I believe that Darin is impacting future generations of 'Kidd's', as a result of being such an extraordinary role model to his own. His legacy will have a profound impact on these future Big Dreamers, as they go about the world sharing what they've learned. Even when he feels he messes up with his kids, he continually asks for forgiveness and always takes 100% responsibility for his actions. He lives with higher values and shares he can be an inspiring example for his family, or a warning sign and stumbling block for those around him. Darin wants to be remembered as being a solid role model, one that others emulate. "How you do anything, is how you do everything and I always keep that top of mind," he shares.

I admire the humility in this man, as he struggles to receive my compliments. He's always humbled when experts, authors and highly successful people reach out and share how real he is. With every action he strives for transparency. He is a relatable and highly approachable Big Dreamer. He prefers to share his imperfections and all the areas he stumbles at with others, as he finds valuable learning lessons through these moments. "We don't fail, we either win or learn," he adds.

Five years ago, he had a desire and a dream of becoming a successful franchise owner across the United States. Around the same time, he learned that his previous mentor was launching a new relationship marketing company in the anti-aging space, so he chose to put his franchise on the back burner. Within 40 months of choosing this opportunity, he earned more income than he did in the past 30-40 years working in traditional jobs. All of his past actions, beliefs, failures and set backs prepared him for this new journey. The drive, passion and determination to reprogram his mind through active listening, was finally paying off. The right associations helped instil powerful belief systems that he was meant for more. It gave him a newfound confidence he could create any kind of income he set his mind on. His intention was to become a multiple six-figure income earner, so he knew he had to surround himself with those types of earners and become that person first in his mind.

He was inspired by authors like, Jack Canfield and Mark Victor Hansen, the co-creators of *Chicken Soup for the Soul Series*, and their desire to become $100 million and $1 billion dollar earners, as a result of their belief in attracting people that were earning those amounts. As he continues to develop his financial mindset he believes there are no limits to what he's able to achieve. If he can continue to see and be it in his mind, he knows with sheer certainty it's just a matter of time when it becomes his reality.

He reflects on the power of his own associations. For years, he invested so much time listening to his greatest mentors, Paul J. Meyer, Jack Canfield and John Maxwell, knowing that one day he would share the stage with each of them. He would hang out with these inspiring men in his car, listening to them every chance he had. He immersed his mind into their books and absorbed their inspiration. Years later, his dream was reality! He was face-to-face with some of his greatest mentors. Everything began to shift in him when he chose to propel his life upwards. "Every time I moved up to a new level in my life, I first believed I could do it," he adds. His decisive pursuit of personal development strengthened and fired up his neurons. "When you are filled with this kind of belief and positivity, you become a contagious ball of enthusiasm," he shares.

Darin had come a long way from his early teen years, when he continually surrounded himself with fighters and would attract negative situations. Today, visionaries surround him; positive and goal oriented people that nourish him. The more intentional he became in attracting positive associations the more his life truly started to shift. The energy he attracted accelerated his success. "I didn't recognize the person in the mirror that I was growing into," he recounted. He was becoming the very man he was seeking. The health and fitness of his mind and body were reaching epic levels of growth. He was no longer stuck in his comfort zone. His life was filled with new and exciting goals. His unseen potential and what he believed was possible blew off the lid that contained him for so many years.

~ Dream Bit ~

Big Dreamers Become The Change They Are Seeking

Big Dreamers know that everyone has the ability to change the course of their lives. The moment they decide that they become the change they are seeking.

Darin's greatest wish for people is to turn their dream machines back on and wipe the dust off. He believes all of humanity, is born with the ability to dream bigger. "It's not an ability that pops up in just a few of us, it lives in all of us," he adds. "By the time a child reaches first grade, they have been told no over 40,000 times and yes only 5,000 times," he shares. As a society, we do very little to nurture the Big Dreamer inside of our children. We transcend so many of our own fears into the minds of our children and condition them to hold back from taking chances and imaging what's truly possible.

"Whatever you vividly imagine, ardently desire, sincerely believe, and enthusiastically act upon... must inevitably come to pass, is a quote by billionaire Paul J. Meyer, that I love," shares Darin. Everyday, he closes his eyes and visualizes the future he is manifesting. He created it in his mind and in time his body will catch up to that vision. He believes in this creative process and recognizes, the right actions and stronger associations will accelerate his success. He shares that the more goal-oriented his actions are on a daily basis the more he'll drive his vision forward. He's a big fan of creating 'dream boards' to support his vision. He laughingly shares that, years ago you wouldn't find him creating and using these kinds of success tools. "I thought it was for kindergarten kids," he adds. He now believes in the power of infusing his mind with positive and supportive visuals that magnetize what he's seeking in his life. This highly and effective success principle, opened up his mind to opportunities he wouldn't have noticed in the past. He understands the power of his subconscious, in bringing the things that matter most to the forefront. "If you don't know where you're going, then any road can easily take you off track," he shares. "Even a world-class archer can miss their target, if you blind fold them and spin them around," he adds. The key message here is that creating a vision board, helps you get clear on what you want to create and experience in your life. Taking action on the goals that are aligned with your vision helps you fixate on your target.

Big Dreamers Spend Time Getting Clear

Big Dreamers are clear on what they want to experience. They don't leave anything to chance. They first decide what they want most and then take powerful action to pursue it. They create meaningful goals, which are aligned with their vision and they act on their inspired thoughts.

Some of the questions that he asked himself when he started turning on his dream machine were:

- Where do I want to travel?
- Where do my family and I want to live?
- What car do I want to drive?
- How much money do I want to earn?
- What would I purchase?
- How do I want to spend my time?
- What charities do I want to give to?

When he creates a vision board, he gets crystal clear on what he's putting down on paper. Then he starts to dream bigger and places a significant emotional attachment to it. He focuses his brain's energy on telling it what he wants to attract. "When you tell your brain what you really want then you don't miss opportunities you normally would. That's why I crystallize my thoughts in my mind," he shares. When he became clear on where he wanted to go, what he desired to do, and how he wanted to live; he strengthened his belief system. The things that used to seem like obstacles eventually faded away out of sight and out of mind. He learned how to leap towards, what he wants most in life. The challenges he experiences along his journey are simply seen as necessary hurdles that he needs to leap over now.

He had an exalted mission to replace older habits with successful ones. He shares how easy it is for him, to get into a negative state and let that energy expand. He still has to fight his negative self talk through affirmations and focus on positive thinking. He attributes his success in creating a new attitude that opens his mind and helps him embrace a new philosophy for viewing the world. He embraced new associations and daily personal development that helped him strengthen his inner-belief. He focused on new ways of listening, thinking and speaking to himself and to others. He liberated himself out of his comfort zone by getting comfortable with being uncomfortable. "I had to find a way to turn off the multiple distractions, as I reached new success levels," he recounts. He learned the art of prioritization by making time for the right stuff. He learned how to say no to others and to energy sucking items, and yes to only the right actions.

What is possible for Darin moving forward, I asked? "Everyday my belief is growing stronger and stronger and my vision is getting bigger and bigger," he shares. He believes there are no limits to the reach of his message and his inspiration. Through his alignment with social media experts, he's confident in his ability to impact so many more people. The confirmation he receives everyday from world-class authors and publishers, strengthens his belief and confidence that he's on the right path.

As he continues to expand on his success, he shares with me that he will always lead from the heart. "It's never about me, I know where I've come from and I will always feel a great sense of humility for where I've landed," he shares. He believes, like most human beings, he has only scratched the surface for what is truly possible. He recognizes the floodgates are getting ready to open in the most positive way and his belief in his dream will impact so many lives.

I love how people can relate to Darin. He's an everyday person, who decided to do extraordinary things. He wants to inspire others to be more, do more and have more with their one precious life. Like me, he believes, ordinary people can achieve the impossible if they are just given that spark. With Darin being the match, I believe he will light the way and help thousands of people turn their dream machines back on. "If Darin Kidd can do it, you can do it and that's the truth," he later noted. He believes in his story and when you are in his presence, you can feel his energy, passion and humility resonating from his heart. With every presentation he makes, he strives to transfer his belief onto the audience members that may not have it, yet. "I want them to borrow my belief, until they feel strong enough to find their own," he shares.

He is as authentic as they come. He believes his approach has the power to travel around the world and impact so many lives. He is very active on social media and it's not difficult to find him doing a series of live trainings on Facebook or Periscope. He shares with me how humbled he is to receive messages from so many people that tell him he has changed their lives.

Darin shares a story, how the littlest actions can have a negative or lasting positive impact on people. He was in Richmond, Virginia a few months back and two ladies were standing behind him in line. He decided to purchase their coffee. He just wanted to deliver this one small act of kindness that day. All he asked them to consider was paying it forward. Months passed by, and to his surprise, one of these ladies discovered him on social media. She then shared a video of him and his family with a beautiful comment about how his small act of kindness inspired her to pay it forward. It makes you wonder how many acts of kindness rippled out that day across Virginia as a result of his action. "The epiphany I had was, imagine if I had treated these ladies rudely and the impact that action might have had instead" he shares.

~Dream Bit ~
Big Dreamers Are Difference Makers

Big Dreamers are difference makers with a goal of creating a ripple effect that will benefit the greater good of all mankind. Big Dreamers act in total alignment with their life purpose. Every action is intended to support others.

He believes no matter what level your education is, or what background you have, or your level of success; we all have an ability to help others by making a difference. "We all have unique gifts that we can contribute to this world," he shares. His goal is to help people become the best version of themselves. "Before I can impact others, I want to become the best version of myself," he adds. This is something he works on everyday.

His greatest wish for others is to make a conscious choice to never settle for a mediocre life. He encourages others to take action and not wait, like he did for so many years of his life. He doesn't want others to experience the regret of someday like his Dad before him. He believes you can start today from anywhere by just committing to being more and working on yourself through personal development. "What is the one thing you can start today that will help you be better and move your life forward?" He shares some suggestions.

Step 1: The first step is deciding what you want and making a list of goals that you want to achieve. "If you don't know where you're going then any road will take you off course," he shares. "You can't hit a target that you can't see."

Step 2: The second step is to map out your goals and desires; and transfer the emotion into a dream board, which will be a visual representation of your goals. The key is to go into as much detail with your dreams and your goal setting as you possibly can.

Step 3: The third step is to take daily action in generating the momentum towards moving your goals forward. Recognize the daily actions that seem to have no direct impact in the moment, but are actually compounding below the surface with an immense ability to impact your future. Similarly, choosing to procrastinate will just as easily compound and impact your future in an adverse way. Everyday, we are faced with thousands of thoughts that affect our choices and every choice impacts the growth or decline, in all areas of our lives, relationships, careers, finances and our inner-happiness.

"My everyday message to people is to be positive. Be encouraged by working on your attitude and your belief," he adds. Pay closer attention to the associations in your life and the people you hang around with as they are either bringing you up or taking your life energy down. Pay attention to what you are listening to and reading, in order to filter out the noise (unwanted sound) in your life.

What he wants to be remembered for is not just talking the talk, but that he walked the walk. That he put God and his family first in his life. He wants others to know he did as much good as he could to as many people as he could reach in his lifetime. He wants to be remembered as being a difference maker, who contributed to making the world a better place. He wants to know his life made a lasting and positive impact on future generations. Years ago, Darin only thought changing himself would be a dream come true. Now, after impacting thousands of people, he believes that millions more can be impacted by his story and message. He is one determined "Kidd" and I believe he can accomplish anything he sets his mind to.

189

~ A Dedication from Darin's wife Cheryl Kidd ~

To my husband, Darin, you dream not only for yourself, but for everyone that is privileged enough to be a part of your life. You never let the details stand in your way. Thank you for creating a "Dream" life for us.

Big Dreamers

DECIDE WHAT YOU WANT MOST, TAKE ACTION AND GO GET IT!

~ Gerry Visca

7. DALE MUNGER
PASSION + PURPOSE

"Watching others win and knowing you've been with them the entire way is truly priceless. There's a certain feeling that comes over you when you help others achieve greatness that can't be measured or explained." ~ Dale Munger

Dale Munger *exists* to change peoples lives. He is on a mission to redefine his family name and create a legacy that will impact generations to follow. Growing up, his family struggled to make ends meet. Both of his parents worked three jobs just to stay afloat. His family lived, along with his father's mother, in a tiny back room of a house. Times were tough and Dale was constantly being uprooted to move every 3 to 4 years. When Dale was only 12, his father suffered a heart attack. He was hospitalized, but his family all anticipated he would return home. Unfortunately, this was not the case, and he sadly passed away while in hospital. Dale shared with me the difficulty that followed his father's death and how he felt lost in his teen years without a dad in his life. There were times he just didn't want to go to school. He blamed the world for his hurt, anger and depression. He felt as if no one understood what he was going through.

When his mother passed just seven years later, at the age of 19, it rocked him to his core. He questioned the existence of God and everything around him. "How could this happen to me?" he shares. He began taking on a defiant persona and an attitude against the world. Your teenage years are difficult enough without having to lose both parents. Fortunately, his high school girlfriend Vanessa guided him through these turbulent times. She was his sweetheart since the age of 16. She was an anchor for the storm that raged inside him. Her energy helped him navigate a new course and outlook on the world. She helped him release his anger, so he could embrace the love he deserved. With her love and support he was able to appreciate the time he shared with his mother. "Many kids grow up without any parents in their lives, I'm grateful for the time I had with her," he shares. His healing had begun and through gratitude he was able to move past his own emotional state by embracing his loss.

Big Dreamers like Dale, realize they're not isolated from the collective energy of the world. In the absence of both parents, he was able to embrace the gift of time with his mother and the love he experienced from Vanessa. He learned to live with a power of gratitude, a trait that would serve him well years later.

Embracing a mindset of gratitude during the most challenging times of his youth opened up his world. He began living with this energy on a daily basis. He didn't fixate on what was missing in his life, but rather, shifted his mindset to one of abundance. Through the power of gratitude, he was able to veer his consciousness and receive love for everything and everyone around him.

~ Dream Bit ~
Big Dreamers See The Greatness In Every Situation

Big Dreamers live with gratitude when faced with challenging situations. They learn to discipline their reaction in any given situation by making a list of what they are grateful for. Big Dreamers harness this power and attract extraordinary people and opportunities their way. They influence their behaviour and shape the outcome of their lives.

Dale's challenging times transformed into powerful lessons. "I believe I needed to go through this time and experience everything in order to shape the character and person I am today," he shares. Through these earlier experiences he realized that every reaction and thought is a choice.

~ Dream Bit ~
Big Dreamers Transfer Challenge Into Growth

Big Dreamers recognize that challenge and discomfort are just a way of life. It's how we respond in any given moment that makes the difference and impacts the outcomes. Big Dreamers take 100% responsibility for the way they show up. Instead of allowing their emotions to control them, they get better at learning from their emotions and using their emotions as a GPS.

It was through these earlier life lessons that he began to look at every situation as a great teaching opportunity. "I started asking myself what is the lesson I am meant to learn from this situation," he adds. He knew by embracing the lessons, he would avoid repeating the same situations. It's the willingness to embrace the teachings in any given moment that gives rise to new opportunities.

Looking back, he's filled with gratitude for his childhood experiences. He learned his amazing work ethic from his parents. "No matter how hard they worked, my parents encouraged my siblings and I to play sports," he shares. His parents both worked night shifts and his dad was a musician. It wasn't unusual for his dad to return home at 3:00 a.m. in the morning. "My dad had a real passion for music and he taught me to have things in life that you are willing to make sacrifices for," he adds.

"I chose to value the time I had with my parents. I've come to see it as an incredible gift," he shares. "So many people, continue to suffer, as a result of not being able to embrace the gifts from their past," he adds. Choosing a positive way to view our world takes effort and focus. Our natural state is to channel our thoughts to the negative aspects of a challenging situation. When we choose love over fear, we are able to fill our minds with positivity. "It makes me wonder, how people can bring positive energy into their lives when they are continually holding themselves back with negativity," he adds.

At the age of 19, it certainly wasn't all sunshine and roses; it was Dale against the world. "At the time, all I could think was, if there is a God then why would he take away my parents from me," he shares. Listening and knowing the level of his faith, I instantly had flashes of God sending him an angel of love and light, to embrace him during these turbulent years. I believe we're all meant to define a great purpose in our lives and that it's often revealed to us when we face our greatest challenges. It's the most strenuous times in our lives that we choose to rise up, and embrace the teachings and the gifts around us. *God only sends us angels* is a mantra I've lived by my whole life. Vanessa served as Dale's angel. She was his candle during his darkest hours.

I love how he's able to surrender his ego and share his vulnerability with me, as I take him through this journey into his past. This is the energy and the intention for this chapter, to serve as a piece of inspiration. I don't know what time this is for you, or what your state of mind is, but it's my intention to inject a new level of belief in you through Dale's inspiration and life journey. We are always being sent angels to help us stay the course and live our purpose. Every moment is a choice to rise above a challenge and choose to become something different. Without discomfort in your life you cannot grow and growth is the only evidence of life. When we collectively choose to create a world inspired, we will elevate the human race to a new plateau. We will replace fear with love, hopelessness with happiness, discomfort and despair with promise and purpose.

Vanessa gave him the space to share what he was feeling in his heart. She intuitively understood the best way to help him was by creating the space for him to process what he was experiencing. The bigger realization was that the death of his parents was out of his control and no amount of blame and personal responsibility would serve him. Vanessa offered a fresh perspective at a time when he needed it most. Sometimes that's all we need, a new way of looking at a situation in order to change it. One of my greatest mentors, the late, Dr. Wayne Dyer shares, "when you choose to change the way you look at things, that's when things change." Dale had created a powerful success habit, at an early age, as a result of remaining open and looking for the lesson in every situation.

I think the insights and lessons from Dale's story, can teach us to move ourselves through life's circumstances and not be defined by them.

~ Dream Bit ~

Big Dreamers Embrace Their Imperfection

Big Dreamers channel their imperfection by choosing to be proactive with their actions. They understand that giving their energy to a situation by instantly reacting to it means they are losing their power. Instead of instantly countering a negative situation, they take the time to process the energy and retain their inner-power.

Dale learned at a young age how to be less reactive to challenging situations. I think one of the greatest challenges, our current generation faces is that we don't let them face discomfort. We shield them from the realities of life and what makes us truly human. We don't want our children to experience the pain and the suffering we went through, but how is this serving them? If they do not experience pain and suffering how will they approach the bigger challenges in their future? Our next generation, will face some of the toughest challenges in the history of our time. Think about it; terrorism is on the rise, countries are facing greater economic depressions than ever before, and we're on the brink of extinction due to global warming.

Big Dreamers like Dale, are masters at traversing difficult events. He embraced challenge and discomfort, but he didn't let these circumstances prevent him from reaching new levels of success. As humans, we are going to feel sad and disconnected from a challenging situation, but it's how you choose to look at the energy that changes its state. You can let the challenge take its hold on you and gain momentum through feelings of anger, resentment, fear, or you can choose to change the way you look at the situation in order to change it for the better.

I admire how Dale moved himself through his earlier life challenges with a simple, yet highly effective strategy. It is something that any of us can learn to master. It just takes practice and catching ourselves in the moments that challenge appears. I often coach people to avoid reacting to a negative situation. The moment you do, you only give away your energy and power. The key is to pause and say, "Isn't that interesting." Look for the teaching in the moment. What can you learn from it? What if you don't respond, what will happen? Think back to the times, you got very emotional from a negative attack at you. Did you instantly react? If so, the situation probably escalated as a result of you feeding it.

In his early 20's, Dale started working for corporations and large construction companies. As he moved up in the corporate ranks, he noticed that hard work ethic didn't really matter in Corporate America. He witnessed friends and colleagues, being laid off or let go, even after years of giving really great service to the company. He knew if the market was affected then he was just a number, regardless of his work ethic. He disliked being in that kind of vulnerable situation for the rest of his life. He was a Big Dreamer and was compelled to express his passion like his Dad. Something inside of him knew he wasn't interested in building someone else's dream.

~ Dream Bit ~

Big Dreamers Build Their Own Dreams

Big Dreamers take 100% responsibility for creating and fuelling their own dreams. They don't place their future in someone else's hands. They believe in the currency of their time and they are not prepared to sell it to others.

He continued to shift to other corporate positions. "I started in the dungeons, the lowest level, located in the basement," he recounted. Eventually, through hard work and persistence he worked his way up and out from customer service to design. He never allowed himself to get comfortable in his current role though. He wasn't willing to settle, and was always looking to progress and get himself out of the dungeons. He embraced a winning attitude and was continually open to better opportunities and defining new milestones. He believed in himself and in his abilities to achieve any goal he set his mind to.

~ Dream Bit ~

Big Dreamers Get Comfortable With Being Uncomfortable

Big Dreamers get comfortable with being uncomfortable by introducing discomfort into their lives. Big Dreamers know that our minds are conditioned to remain in a comfortable state, so they challenge it.

Every new level he reached he was faced with a challenging employer. Even though he didn't care much for his superiors, he never criticized or embraced a negative attitude towards them. Instead, he chose to look for the lessons in these situations. "My co-workers continually complained that their boss was to blame for their lack of success in life, so I decided to embrace a different perspective," he adds. He recognized he was a Big Dreamer and it was just a matter of time before he could step into creating his dream life. He chose to embrace the temporary challenge of working for difficult employers. He accepted the corporate culture, as a contrast, for what he didn't want in his life. His journey through Corporate America provided valuable lessons, however, as he now knew he wanted to experience a different way of existing in the world. It was this kind of openness that attracted new opportunities his way.

It was a friend of his, who worked for a mortgage business that shared an opportunity for Dale to become his own boss. He jumped at the chance and spent the time to become a mortgage appraiser with his wife. "My friend was prepared to flow, all of his clients our way, in order to help make the transition smoother for us," he shares. He worked as an appraiser part-time, while still being employed full-time in his corporate job. "I knew I would either be let go, as a result of downsizing, or get into trouble for moonlighting. Either way, I didn't care about the outcome, I was finally taking 100% responsibility for creating our own future," he adds.

After time, his part-time appraisal business started taking off. He knew the more he focused on it, the more it would expand, so he decided to offer his full-time employer two months notice. "My boss had no interest in giving me any more time and gladly accepted my resignation. I was now a free man and the sky was the limit," he recounted. "I felt as if there was nothing holding me back from soaring in my own business," he adds. During this time, the housing market was growing and his optimistic outlook to expand was moving along. Life was good and he was becoming comfortable with his newfound success.

The 2008 economic recession hit North America hard. Over the next 2 years, Dale and Vanessa struggled to stay afloat. Despite his best efforts the economy was like a tornado sweeping in and destroying everything in its path; and they were at the centre of it all. Everything they worked for over the past few years was gone. The recession took a financial and emotional toll on him and his family. They couldn't afford to keep up with the car and house payments. "I felt I had reached the lowest point in my life, by having to empty our kids room just to pay a few bills," he recalls. He has since shared this memory with thousands of people, yet the pain still triggers him emotionally. He is a provider and all of his energy is directed towards providing for his family. So, sitting on the floor of his kid's empty room, where he use to hold and sing his kids to sleep, rocked him to his core. He remembers looking around in wonderment, "I couldn't believe what I had just done," he shares.

To add to the discomfort, just a few months earlier one of his boys was diagnosed with Type 1 Diabetes, and they didn't have insurance to cover the treatment. He once again, felt like he was in hell. He knew from past experience if he chose to sit still though that he would remain in hell. "In that moment, I decided to pray to God for a miracle to appear," he recounts. Days later, the phone rang and another angel was sent to Dale. His best friend, Danny Gasemy, was on the line. Danny invited them to his home the following week to preview a new opportunity. "If it wasn't for Vanessa attending that meeting we wouldn't be where we are today," he shares. He had been praying for a miracle and suddenly there was his friend reaching out to him.

~ Dream Bit ~

Big Dreamers Are Open

Most people listen with the intent to reply instead of listening with the intent to understand the bigger picture in front of them. Big Dreamers see the bigger picture and realize that although it might just be an idea, the energy can lead to the development of other ideas.

203

The decision to bring Vanessa to meet Danny and listen to the opportunity was his way of opening his heart and not letting the challenge of his financial situation get the best of him. "I was so excited to learn about the opportunity that Danny tapped into," he recounts. He remembered Danny was struggling financially as well, so he was curious as to what he had stumbled upon. After listening and previewing Danny's presentation, he thought his friend was out of his mind! "Skin care, why the hell would we want to sell skin care," he remembers thinking. He looked over at Vanessa thinking she was likely ready to leave, but to his surprise, she jumped out her seat and shouted, "This is it Dale! This is what we've been waiting for, this is the big one!" She couldn't contain herself. "What did she see that I didn't?" The start up fee was only $500, but to Dale it might as well have been $50,000. Times were so tough; he had just finished emptying his son's room to make a few dollars, so how would they be able to afford this? Vanessa looked at him and with wide-open eyes confidently shared, "We can't afford to miss out on this opportunity, so we're going to give it everything we've got!"

A couple days later, they borrowed the money from friends, signed up and got straight to work. Using the product made him an instant believer in only a few short days. He believed in his wife and trusted in her confidence and intuition.

~ Dream Bit ~

Big Dreamers Lead With An Open Heart

Big Dreamers lead with their heart. They believe in something bigger than themselves. They know there is something far greater at work in the universe and they remain open to this energy and inner knowing. It guides their actions and helps them access the creative side of their minds.

He believed the temporary discomfort they were experiencing was just that, temporary. Even though they were experiencing a turbulent time in their lives, he believed this change was intended to open up a much wider path. "I knew that if our belief was strong, that others would soon see the same opportunity that Vanessa embraced," he recounted. "I knew that without a rock-solid belief people would read my energy like an open book," he adds. Belief is the fuel that drives him. He has an authentic energy and wears his emotions on his sleeve.

He was compelled to meet up and connect with the founder of the company. Dale is a connector and what connects him most to others is his willingness to share his heart. He poured out his heart that day and to his surprise the founder responded with the words that he needed to hear. "He hit me with some powerful words when he said, to get up, I have to look up, and if I'm giving up, then I should go home and tell my boys I'm giving up on them," he recounts. This cemented his belief in the opportunity that Danny had presented to them. "What I knew for certain was that I was not ready to give up on my boys," he shares. This energy ignited the fuse and he was ready to launch the Big Dreamer within.

He realized his family was in hell, but he wasn't prepared to sit there. Forward was now his only direction. The word "stop" was no longer in his vocabulary. He was a crusader on a mission of prosperity and growth. Visions of redefining the Munger name filled him with purpose.

205

~ Dream Bit ~

Big Dreamers Ignite Their Potential

Big Dreamers tap into their unlimited potential. They don't let rejections take them off course, for they know it is part of the ride. They keep their head up and don't let the energy of their current situation become their only reality. They fixate on a new reality and take inspired action. They create a greater sense of urgency for their lives.

He was not ready to give up on his family. After meeting with the founder of this new company he set his sights on success. He raised the sails, keyed in the course and set out to create a new legacy. He used the energy from that meeting to fuel his daily habits. "I declared to myself, if I don't give this opportunity 100% I would have to tell my boys I was quitting on them," he shares. He created a new sense of urgency for his life.

He was aware of the realities of his current situation. He and his wife were penniless, and their child needed insulin to survive. "I had an exalted purpose to implement change in my life and I knew the only way out was to look up and do something new," he shares. By embracing their circumstances as a catalyst for growth, they were able to propel themselves forward with greater momentum.

This is a powerful insight. Using your current situation as the ignition and spark to ignite change in your life! When you decide what you want most in life things often need to change. When you embrace the change and look for the positivity within the adversity, everything changes. Avoid becoming defined by your past or your current circumstances. Instead, choose to continually define yourself and the life you desire to create in the present moment.

~ Dream Bit ~

Big Dreamers Decide What They Want and Why They Want It!

Big Dreamers lead all areas of their lives knowing Why. They don't get hung up on the How, but rather connect to their hearts through the power of Why. It drives their actions and gives them clarity and focus. Big Dreamers realize they are born as powerful creators with an ability to focus on what they want most.

Dale dreamed of prosperity and success; and believed he could create it. I admire his dedicated enthusiasm for driving change in his life. He is filled with passion and purpose. "To be successful, you have to turn off the noise. If I listened to my friends, Vanessa and I wouldn't be where we are today," he shares. Shutting off that noise is one of the biggest challenges Big Dreamers must overcome. It's easy to be swayed by what the rest of the world thinks you should be doing with your life. Dale shared a great analogy, where a bunch of cars are stopped in the left lane at a traffic light. He said that he saw all these cars following one another and that the right lane was completely empty, so he chose it and passed everyone by. He later shares that, "this is how most people live, they follow the rest of the cars, instead of carving their own way in the world."

~ Dream Bit ~
Big Dreamers Create Their Own Way

Big Dreamers build their dreams of a better world for themselves and their families. They invest in themselves and avoid buying into other people's opinions. They don't follow the status quo. They put on a new lens that helps them see their vision more clearly, so when opportunities and inspiration presents itself they know it's time to act.

He didn't settle on what others saw for his life. He was a passionate crusader who always envisioned himself as a Big Dreamer. It's as if his parents still surrounded him with their energy and it's this energy that pushes him beyond the pain to create a bigger world for his family. He never got hung up on what he couldn't do, but rather, continuously dreamed of a life where he was making a difference in other people's lives. This was the purpose he fixated on and he knew that one day his dream would become a reality. No matter how many times he took a step back, he followed it with four leaps forward. In his mind he was dreaming bigger, believing in himself and in new possibilities.

He focused all of his love, attention and energy towards earning a yearly income of $100,000. He visualized this success by placing a dollar bill on the ceiling above his bed and added a bunch of zeroes to it with a sharpie pen. Everyday, he fixated on that amount and believed he would one day attract this income into his life. He recognized he was worthy of receiving it. To this day, he keeps that $100,000 dollar bill above his head as a reminder of the life he created. His bigger dream is to now attract that kind of income every single month. When it comes to being a Big Dreamer he certainly fits the bill!

~ Dream Bit ~
Big Dreamers Cultivate New Belief Systems

Big Dreamers see opportunity where others only see obstacles. They believe in something bigger than themselves. They experience a different energy in the world and it is a positive force that propels them forward. They recognize that everything is a choice and they sift out what no longer serves them. They always remain open to bigger possibilities.

No matter what adversities he experienced in his life he knew he was always a millionaire. He knew it deep in his heart and he shared this intention with everyone. No one else needed to get his dream; he just knew he had to cultivate a mind of prosperity. It may not have been a reality, however, in his mind he was living his success. He just needed to believe, take action and catch up with his vision.

~ Dream Bit ~
Big Dreamers Believe In Unseen Forces

Big Dreamers believe the laws of the universe are governed by a series of unseen forces, which are forever in motion. They are spiritual in nature and inspired with new possibilities. It is their belief that they are meant for more, which makes them a Big Dreamer.

His past actions, thoughts, and beliefs attracted the friends and opportunities that propelled his life forward. He remembers when he was around 20 years old, a very successful friend, shared with Dale that he would become very successful in life as a result of his positive outlook. He still remembers the feeling those words had on him. He carried that belief with him throughout his life. He knew he was destined to be a strong and thriving leader. He was to pass on his knowledge for success to thousands of others. Sometimes that is all we need to elevate our success. It is the belief from a fellow human being, who notices untapped potential within us.

Throughout his early 20's, he learned to nurture the power of visualization. He recalls how he would see himself behind the steering wheel of his brand new Lexus, while he was driving an old Toyota Highlander with rear windows that didn't even work! He never let the reality of his current situation cloud his vision for the life he dreamed of creating. Once, he visited a Lexus dealership, cut out their logo from a brochure and pasted it onto the steering wheel of his old Toyota. Talk about visualization!

~ Dream Bit ~

Big Dreamers See The Vision Clearly In Their Minds

Big Dreamers like Nicola Tesla and Thomas Edison saw the end result of what they were creating years before they realized their dream. They implanted the idea like a seed of potential within their subconscious. Big Dreamers recognize that daily visualization, when stimulated through higher levels of positivity and emotion can ignite their dreams. Big Dreamers are masters at creating priorities and focusing their energy on the things that truly matter.

It's easy to look at Dale's current life and assume everything was always sunshine and roses. We often don't see what's behind the curtain or hiding back stage. Not only did both of his parents die before he turned 20; Dale barely graduated from high school. He never let his lack of education stop him from driving his life forward through hard work and discipline though. He is a competitive man by nature and thrives when challenged. He always remained open and focused on personal growth. He never shied away from developing himself. He never feared heading into the unknown and refused to adhere to the status quo.

With an unwavering belief in himself, his work ethic and his passion, he was able to build his success. "With an ounce of doubt, I would have been out! It's the belief in something bigger, that's going to get you through," he shares. "Life throws you curve balls, but in baseball, it eventually curves in and crosses the plate, and you can hit it out of the park; if you just wait patiently for it," he adds. He never let a challenge intimidate him out of the batters box. He approached all of the curve balls that life threw him in the same manner. He stayed the course by sinking his feet firmly into the ground, fixated on the end prize, and made a conscious choice to hit the ball out of the park.

Experiencing this man's passion, I shared with him my new term for this energy, "Munger Motivation!" Dale laughingly responds, "I love it!"

I was curious what he would say to his 19-year-old self, given the chance? Perplexed by the intensity and emotion of this question, he paused before revealing the life lessons he would share:

- **Don't fall into the trap of believing in other people's opinions.** No matter what happens to you in life, whatever circumstances try to bring you down, don't believe in it! Know that it's a temporary pain that will subside.

- **Outwork the person next to you.** Replace the doubt with new levels of belief. Don't restrict the growth of your future by the limiting your belief. Don't think that you are not good enough, talented enough or strong enough. Believe that you are worth it. Replace the negativity with action, discipline and hard work.

- **Don't live with the pain of regret.** Refuse to limit yourself and your potential. See yourself as a Big Dreamer with an ability to create a new reality for your life. When faced with difficult choices, ask yourself how the outcomes of not taking action will impact you and your family.

- **Participate in your own rescue.** You are the only one that can make the changes you are seeking. When you decide to make a significant impact on your life that's when everything changes. Be willing to become the change you wish to see in others and in the world around you. Wishing and hoping that others will make the change is a waste of energy. You cannot expect others to change since it's out of your control. Look in the mirror and declare to yourself with certainty that you are ready and willing to change your life. Put 100% effort forward and do the work, everyday, inch by inch, to move your life forward.

- **Love everyone around you.** You never know if your paths will cross again someday. Avoid burning bridges, even in the toughest moments. Embrace everyone and everything as a great teacher, who is meant to help you move forward.

- **Build your dream, not someone else's.** It's far easier to live with the pain of building your dream than spending 20 years of your life's energy building someone else's!

- **Never be a follower.** Avoid being average. Blaze your own trail, as you will experience greater levels of fulfillment. Avoid the comfort of staying with the pack and the safety of not standing out. It only leads to living a mediocre existence.

- **Decide what you want most.** If you want something bad enough you will receive it. You have to desire it in the same way you crave oxygen.

- **Don't let fear dominate your thoughts.** Focus on reconditioning your mind to become what you are seeking. Every time that life attempts to get you down, pull your "Munger Motivation" card and tell yourself, you are a winner! You won't stop fighting for what matters most and for the dreams you are pursuing.

- **Read self-help books.** Commit to reading a few pages of a very positive book everyday. This habit strengthens the mind through personal development. The more you read, the better you become for yourself and your family. This seemingly insignificant habit is what drives the success of all Big Dreamers.

~ Dream Bit ~
Big Dreamers Embrace Hard Work

Big Dreamers don't shy away from hard work and they use their talents and gifts to propel them forward. They believe in possibility and they replace older conditioned habits with new successful ones.

Dale didn't let his shyness stop him from meeting new people; instead he cultivated a new success habit and mindset. "Vanessa even helps by literally pushing me into crowds of people," he laughs. He was prepared to convert his shyness into becoming a stronger leader, first by leading himself, then others.

What enabled him to attract success the first year of their new skin care business was his belief that he deserved it, and that it was possible. Dale posted positive visuals and messages throughout his home and in his car reaffirming that he was a winner and a warrior. "To this day, I surround myself with messages like, I am going to bless somebody today," he shares. He attributes much of his success to this positive mindset. He never stops believing in himself, his family and in the people he serves as a global leader. "Any ordinary person walking into my home would immediately think that I'm crazy seeing all of these positive notes everywhere," he shares.

Big Dreamers

~ Dream Bit ~
Big Dreamers Surround Themselves With Positive and Visual Clues

Big Dreamers embrace the power of positive reinforcement through visual clues and key messages implanted into their subconscious. They continually surround themselves with this kind of energy. They live with tremendous joy and understand it fuels their passions. They avoid negativity in all areas of their lives.

"Even though I was focused on pursuing my goals with determination it was easy to allow others to pull me down to their level," he shares. His family and friends told him that his new vision of being a network-marketing leader would never work. He experienced ridicule and embarrassment from those closest to him, but he didn't let them hold him down or stop him from dreaming bigger.

We will always encounter others that try to bring us down. It is a part of nature. In a bucket of crabs for instance, there is always one crab that tries to escape. It wants to challenge the status quo and leave the group. Sound familiar? Well, the other crabs say no to that, and do everything they can to stop that crab from escaping. If the crab continues to make a second and third attempt at freedom the other crabs will literally break its claws.

If you have ever tried to break free, I'm sure you can relate to this feeling of defeat. We all experience people in our lives that at some point or another try to stop us from experiencing freedom. They seem to crawl up when we decide to leave our comfort zones and dream bigger. The key is to continually live in a state of growth, like Dale. He creates even bigger goals and drives every action through his driving purpose to inspire change in peoples lives. He has given himself permission to dream again, and harnessed the discomfort in his life, by choosing to ignite a fire in his heart. He wasn't prepared to give up on his boys. "I refused to spend another day sitting inside my garage, thinking I couldn't afford to buy my kids medicine," he recounts. He was a renegade and his sheer determination and will to create a new life for his family is what inspires me to publish his story.

Most people will go through life, not really knowing what it means to be alive. It's easier to choose the safe path, even if it takes you to the side of a cliff, than to dream big sometimes! You don't have to wait for the circumstances in your life to become so dire though to move yourself forward. Don't wait for life to become so hard, that you are left with little or no choice. "Unfortunately, I had to hit rock bottom to truly see who I was," he shares. He recognized that even at his lowest point, he only needed to look up in order to get himself out of hell. "Most people might not have hit rock bottom like me, but that's no excuse to live an average life and never give yourself permission to dream bigger," he adds.

~ Dream Bit ~

Big Dreamers Are Filled With Love

Big Dreamers embrace the power of love as an energy source. They choose to act without judgment and share their intentions with the world. They embrace the notion that they are imperfect beings, but pursue higher levels of personal perfection.

I asked Dale what his state of mind was during the most challenging days of his reinvention. He enthusiastically responded, "I love that question! I approached life as if I was preparing for a super bowl championship. How could I make this a competition for myself?" What is your trigger point that will get you into the right action? For Dale, it was his passion for sports and years of training as an athlete that strengthened his mindset. He loved competition and he chose to win at the game of life. When others would tell him he couldn't do it that triggered the competitor inside of him to dream bigger. He made a conscious decision to either die trying or collapse from the exhaustion of playing to win. There was no alternative within his mind, he was a warrior and he knew he had to master the head game. This was his Super Bowl and the arena where he would show the world, the new Munger bloodline. He was fulfilling a life-long dream to create a new family legacy. The end zone represented more than just a touch down it meant something more profound to him. He believed he could be the quarterback and create the playbook of his life.

Listening to Dale share his energy is like witnessing first hand, a transformational shift right before my eyes. He experienced tremendous adversity in his life, yet chose to overcome his obstacles and contribute to the lives of others. I'm reminded of my personal shift years ago, when I made a declaration to take 100% responsibility for the inspirational life I desired to create. Everything had to change, my relationships, my business, my way of seeing the world and myself. I had to train like an athlete and work on my physical, mental, emotional and spiritual energy.

~ Dream Bit ~
Big Dreamers Commit To Change

Big Dreamers commit to serious change and that's when everything in their life changes. They don't waste energy attempting to change others, but rather focus on changing their own mindset. They commit themselves to intense daily personal development.

For Dale, it was about dominating his subconscious mind with new positive thoughts. He knew he had an opportunity to create greater levels of wealth and he wasn't prepared to slow himself down. His competitive nature, and winning spirit, inspired his actions and the way he trained himself. Some of his closest friends joined his team, ran along side him and accelerated his pace for greater end results.

One of his techniques for pushing through the pain is a proven method that many Big Dreamers embrace. When he is feeling challenged or down he gets it out of his head and onto paper, by asking himself, "What am I feeling in this moment?" The very act of writing it down immediately starts to shift his energy. It's this act of writing things out that ignites the creative and intuitive side of our minds. Following that first part of the exercise, Dale then writes on the opposite page what he can do about it. The very act of contemplating and living this question on paper puts you into a positive state within minutes. "The key lesson from this, is to avoid keeping the energy of the emotion inside of your head," he shares. You instantly access the creative side of your brain by asking what you can do about it, and that's a great way to fire up and release the endorphins in your mind.

Big Dreamers

~ Dream Bit ~

Big Dreamers Are Proactive

Big Dreamers employ creative strategies for disciplining their setbacks by immediately transferring the challenge into an opportunity.

They empower themselves daily and harness their power to take control of their lives. Big Dreamers look for the positive in every situation and relish in what they have, not what they lost. They look for the lessons in every adversity and pay it forward. Big Dreamers don't live in a negative space for long, for they understand that this energy breeds more negativity. They shift their vibration from a negative into to a positive state. This energy quickly impacts and inspires everyone around them and attracts greater levels of abundance their way.

I love how he shares an extraordinary example of this technique and life lesson through the recent passing of his 80-year-old Aunt. "I loved her dearly and was very close to her, especially after the passing of my parents," he shares. "I experienced a low energy emotion for over an hour after her passing. However, by using this release method, I was able to instantly shift my energy by writing down all of the positive experiences my family and I shared with her over the years". He appreciated that his boys and his wife had the opportunity to share her energy. Instead of floundering by her passing he celebrated her 80 years of life and the gifts she bestowed onto his whole family.

I see only unlimited possibilities in this man's life. Laughing, he shares with me, "I love how crowds of people at airports choose to go through the same door. I always look for the unopened door and the moment I crack it open, a sea of people come rushing up behind me". He recognizes only doors of opportunity everywhere he goes, and chooses to live his life in a similar way, never following the pack and always cracking open new doors of possibility. His relentless belief in others helps him pave the way for them to succeed.

He is now crossing new thresholds and bridging the borders as he expands his business into other countries. "Imagine how many more lives we can positively influence and contribute to on a global scale," he adds. Dale is ecstatic for his life and filled with passion and curiosity for the human spirit. He is a loyal leader that inspires his team to dream bigger. He doesn't believe in luck and advocates hard work, in order to create significant change in your life. He's focused on touching and contributing to as many lives as possible, and will be regarded as a hard worker who gave more to others so they could dream bigger. He wants to be remembered for rejecting fear by living a life of love. He wouldn't want his family and friends to mourn his loss, but rather, celebrate his extraordinary life, the Munger way.

~ A Dedication from Dale's wife Vanessa Munger ~

Dale Munger always lived with Big Dreams. We have been together since we were 16 years old. He has such a big heart and always loved helping people. Throughout the years, he focused on changing himself through personal development. The number one thing I could give my husband is unconditional love and belief. Whether his plans and ideas where successful or not, supporting him and believing in him, was something I was not going to ever stop doing. My support and belief in him helped us grow stronger as a couple. It strengthened our faith and made us more successful. I love my husband so much and will always have unconditional love, and belief in him. I will stand by his side no matter what. Dale has a heart of gold and it shines and touches everyone he meets. I believe if you want a successful partner in your life, you have to help them shine by believing in them.

IF YOU HAVE NEVER FALLEN YOU HAVE NEVER CHALLENGED YOUR POTENTIAL

~ Gerry Visca

8. Paddy McCracken
FAIL BETTER

"It doesn't matter what happens to you, what matters most, is that you just keep moving yourself forward." ~ *Paddy McCracken*

Paddy McCracken *exists* to inspire others into positive action. Growing up as a young boy he felt very blessed. He was the son of an entrepreneur and was greatly influenced by his parent's hard-work ethic. He spent a majority of his time in his parent's office and was always surrounded by adults. His parents had successfully built 33 restaurants across central Illinois and within the smaller surrounding towns. It was his parent's vision to integrate their restaurant culture within the heart of communities. This is why they chose to locate a great number of their restaurants throughout smaller towns to boost the local economy and help employ local high school students. They were deeply connected to the local infrastructure within these communities.

He was a daddy's boy growing up and loved spending a great deal of time with his father. Today, he proudly refers to him as his hero. He attributes his inspiration of being a Big Dreamer to the influence of his father. When he wasn't in school, he spent a great deal of time with his father, visiting job sites, meeting with bankers, accountants and lawyers. If he wasn't attending a meeting with his father, you could often find him soaking up knowledge, in his father's large office. Paddy was continuously immersed in a world of creativity and entrepreneurialism.

~ Dream Bit ~

Big Dreamers Surround Themselves With Positive Energy

Big Dreamers are energy magnets, and therefore, very protective of their energy. They believe in the power of attraction and they are very selective in who they share their precious energy with. They understand the power of associations. It's not unusual for a Big Dreamer to have a series of positive mentors and protégés simultaneously.

He was raised and educated by a tribe of creative and business professionals. It's the primary reason he never placed a great emphasis on pursuing formal education. He always viewed himself following in the footsteps of his father and becoming a businessman. He was proud of his father and always saw himself surpassing his accomplishments as a tribute to the influence he had on his life. His father served as a powerful benchmark for Paddy's success.

He was inspired by how much his parents gave to their local communities. He loved how pivotal they were in touching the hearts of the communities they served. They focused on being an integral part the local culture and often furnished schools with books and supplies. He witnessed the deep influence his parents had on others and how highly regarded they were by local officials.

~ Dream Bit ~

Big Dreamers Impact The World at Large

Big Dreamers think far beyond themselves. They strive to create inspired tribes and are driven by a deeper purpose. They wake up each day inspired and on fire to contribute their unique gifts with others, for they know they're connected to a greater consciousness.

Throughout his youth, he wasn't a strong reader and struggled in grade school. He had a speech impediment that impacted how he interacted with other kids. His teachers would often mention that they felt Paddy lacked intelligence. In his parent's business world, he was inspired to be more, yet in school, he felt small, insecure and unsure of himself. His struggle continued throughout the later years of high school and college. He was tired and frustrated by the continual need for tutors and just wanted to inspire people like his father. He didn't see his future success being served by formal education, in fact this environment was taking its toll on him. Looking back, he realizes he was seeking a different way of learning. He shares how this discomfort and challenge became a powerful catalyst for influencing his future path and direction. These life events, ignited what he refers to as, "an attitude adjustment", towards embracing personal development.

~ Dream Bit ~

Big Dreamers Invest Deeply In Themselves

Big Dreamers invest energy in doing the right things. They see personal development, as a gateway to the world and to unlocking their greater potential. They read 5-10 pages everyday, and their library is filled with personal development books.

The earlier years of struggling with formal education ignited a new path towards personal development for Paddy. He was continuously surrounded and influenced by business mentors at a young age. In his late teens, he was already aware that generating income didn't have to come from the formal and traditional models that most people choose. He wasn't interested in simply getting a college degree and then working for the rest of his life. He was driven to live among the entrepreneurial giants, like his father.

"When I was around 12 years of age, my parents decided to sell all of their restaurants for a significant amount of money," he shares. The local media had a frenzy with the way this news was positioned, and as a result, these communities became very negative with the hearsay. Paddy was greatly impacted by the publicity, and more importantly the negative portrayal of his parents to the community. "My parents were selfless, and always worked hard to put others first. In this case, they wanted to ensure their partners and associated stakeholders, were taken care of first before they were compensated from the sale," he recounts. These events had a significant impact on him. He suddenly went from being very popular in the community, and in school, to being blacklisted and excluded from his friends. He felt isolated and found himself having to cultivate new friendships.

He began to view friendships, and the concept of loyalty in a whole different way. He found himself questioning the actions of family and friends. "I couldn't understand why they were doing this to us and shunning us out," he adds. Even though he sees this time of his life as a major opportunity for growth, looking back there were also many dark and depressing days he endured.

These challenging times eventually lost their energy and grip on Paddy, yet something deeper emerged in its place. It was a fear of success. He began associating prosperity with being isolated from friends and community. To him, success meant isolation and disconnection. "I thought if I became successful, then, I'm not going to have any loyal friends," he shares. This emotion became the dominating thought in his mind. He didn't just witness the challenges his parents were going through, he also experienced and carried their pain in his heart.

At age 20, he made the decision to drop out of college and pursue life as an entrepreneur. He decided to fulfill a lifelong dream and relocate to California. His up line leadership and mentors lived in California, so he decided being closer to them would allow him to model their success. Paddy was bustling to kick-start his future entrepreneurial success, through his first network marketing opportunity. College no longer served him, or the bigger entrepreneurial life he dreamed of creating for so many years.

In the past, he travelled extensively with his parents to 5 star resorts, so he savoured the thought of travelling and building a global business. He packed up his car and made the move to California, where he apprenticed for the next several years under his mentors.

Life in sunny California wasn't what he thought it would be. Instead of spending time building a business, he found himself, running day-to-day tasks. He eventually quit his job to become a personal assistant and chauffeur to his mentor. While his mentor was busy with being on stage, Paddy was learning the inner-workings and back stage details of the industry.

Aside from the surmountable success his mentor achieved, Paddy was broke and living on $1 dollar chicken sandwiches, barely making enough income to survive. "At the time, I felt lucky that fast food companies came out with a dollar menu," he recounted. He went from having a gas credit card in high school to now scrambling for quarters just to get by. He experienced the highs and lows of life and he now found himself at one of the lowest points. "I was broke and questioning why," he shares. He was working harder than ever before, but he didn't have anything of value and was earning a small annual income of $30K. He eventually had to sell his car just to pay his rent.

I'm impressed with Paddy's ability to see this time of his life as a powerful catalyst. He needed to undergo days of disgust, in order to arrive at a deeper awareness of his potential.

On a positive note, he was able to surround himself with very successful people. Even though he found himself financially challenged, a powerful undercurrent of energy was stirring, and he knew it would eventually carry him on a path of success. "These times represented my bigger personal development days," he shares. "I was learning and incubating how to master powerful success habits, by studying successful people around me," he adds. He developed a keen understanding for the inner-workings and the mindset that drove successful people. He mastered the art of listening and observation; and instead of replying, he was listening with the intent to understand what these successful leaders were sharing with him.

He was fascinated with one particular leader, Jeff Olson, the author of the book titled, *The Slight Edge*. Throughout his mid 20's, he did whatever he could to be in the presence of this powerful and inspiring man. "I loved listening to all of his past success stories, how he nurtured the people around him, and how be built his past companies," he recounted. More and more, Paddy was sensing and experiencing a new kind of aura of success. As a result, he gazed above his current challenges, by developing a stronger mindset of prosperity. His current reality was no longer the one he saw or what he felt in his heart. He dreamed and imagined something more. His dream machine was cranked way up, and he saw himself leading and inspiring teams across the globe. He envisioned supporting local communities, like the way his father taught him for so many years.

~ **Dream Bit** ~

Big Dreamers Focus On Creating New Realities

Big Dreamers are deep thinkers. Some people see them as having an intense energy.
They continually reflect on their life and the deeper purpose driving their existence.
They continually look up and are inspired by a deeper calling.

"I looked in the mirror and told myself, Paddy, you have been raised too well to be at this low point in your life," he shares. He was raised in a world of considerable success, his family, pillars in their community, so how could his life amount to simply this? It was this knowledge that created a negative energy and a dark shadow that haunted him for years. "You deserve more and you should be more, were the words that filled my mind," he recounted. He was determined to crush the demons that held him back from dreaming bigger and becoming the person he knew deep in his heart he was meant to be. He knew he wasn't serving the world by simply existing and hoping to survive.

He surrounded himself with extraordinary people in California, dreaming bigger than ever before, and learning new success skills. He was ready for success and ready to play bigger. At age 29, his growing belief in himself, attracted and opened the doors for a new and successful opportunity.

~ Dream Bit ~
Big Dreamers Create A Mindset For Success

Big Dreamers do the work on themselves daily. They seek out and model successful people. They move through challenges, a day at a time, by remaining focused on the outcomes they're creating. They don't waste time in trying to change people and past circumstances. They focus on changing their own mind.

Dreaming big was now a part of his daily success regime. He always knew he would be successful; there was never any doubt in his mind and he believed it was just a matter of time. Even though he was not driven by material possessions, he knew he could have whatever he dreamed was possible. He is not surprised by his current success in the global organization he built. Everything he has attracted into his life, is the result of his strong will and belief in himself.

He was driven to push beyond a fear of success. While in California, whether he was recruiting for his own business, or for one of his mentors, he was instrumental at adding value to people's lives. This was a strong asset that he continued to cultivate within himself and others. He intentionally positioned himself out of his comfort zone by traversing multiple industries. These different industries, sharpened his soft skills, like networking and cold calling prospects. He learned the art of selling and moving past his fears. Even though he was living cheque to cheque, he was surrounded by success, while living in beautiful California.

He was never a big fan of formal education, like his Grandmother was; yet he savoured learning and personal development. It was his persistent commitment to growth that continually attracted successful mentors and leaders from multiple industries. He moved about his daily life, with a positive attitude, and was fun to be around. He always found a way to survive and rise above his current situation.

He recognizes the powerful lessons he learnt from the most challenging times in his life. "It was as if I was meant to go through them and develop myself," he shares. He was constantly learning leadership skills, he knew, would one day take him to whole new levels.

Big Dreamers Are Always Present To The Moment

Big Dreamers harness the power of being present and knowing it will impact their future. Your greatest growth is below the surface, usually the one you can't see. It's fuelled by intention, belief and desire and when you add persistence and discipline, that's when you ignite your greatest growth.

His new school of personal development became his associations with industry leaders. Whether he was walking someone back to his or her room, or hanging out with leaders by the pool, he was taking notes and developing himself everyday. He didn't allow his current financial circumstances to become his only reality. He was a Big Dreamer, and he knew his greatest growth had to first happen below the surface. His time would come.

He was quickly learning, that it wasn't about the product or the company, but rather the person that you can become along the way. "The skills I learned during my early 20's, were far more powerful than anything I could have learned at college," he shares. This is not to knock formal education, but it's the following business skills that Big Dreamers learn on the street, which helps them reach new levels of success:

- How to develop the right posture.
- How to create proper follow-ups with people you just met.
- How to type up a professional inquiry letter.
- How to deliver an engaging presentation to future customers and partners.

It's these kinds of skills that Paddy learned to master, by simply choosing to surround himself with incredible and successful people. Every encounter represented an explosive opportunity for growth. "I believed if I stayed the course and continued to focus on my dreams, then the right people and opportunities, would eventually reveal themselves," he recounted. He made the choice to immerse himself in these surroundings and apprentice under successful leaders, whom he respected and modelled.

While living in California, he was involved in a serious accident that created a major setback and tested him in a whole new way. In this car accident an airbag was deployed and it slammed his face back, causing him to lose vision in his right eye. If he didn't have health insurance, he's not sure he would have been able to heal himself from this trauma. He was fortunate to once again, be surrounded by great leaders in their field. Three specialists were caring for him. He had to undergo an $80K surgery on his right eye, just to help restore a portion of his vision and avoid losing his eyesight. To this day, he only has 20% use of his right eye, which affects many of his day-to-day routines, like reading. "I have to be very careful when driving, due to a massive blind spot which is a result of my damaged right eye," he adds.

In sharing this story with me, I am amazed as to how he is able to see the positive even in the most turbulent times. He sees every challenge as an opportunity for growth. He had never experienced any major accidents like this and was now forced to walk around wearing a massive white bandage wrapped around his head and face. Instead of wallowing in self-pity, he was filled with gratitude for having a great physician and several eye specialists that restored a portion of his sight. He was not able to get 100% of his vision back, yet he still felt gratitude, for being surrounded by really great healers. He always knew he would be ok and it was this deeper knowing that helped him feel connected to something bigger.

He felt he was meant to experience these challenges, so he could one day share his inspiring story with others. He knew he was a Big Dreamer, meant to cast his light and inspiration on others. "It doesn't matter what happens to you, what matters most, is you just keep moving yourself forward," he adds.

Growing up Paddy lived on a farm with his family. It was at the farm that he experienced challenging life incidences, from being run over by a horse to being hit by a car. Despite this, he always felt he was protected to fulfill a greater purpose. It's another reason why he gives so much of his time and attention to others. He listens with the intent to understand people, and practices always being present, even at the larger events where he speaks. He really empathises with people, when they share with him, the challenges they live with. He helps people push beyond their current pain by sharing the challenges he had to face, and reminds them of their power to create a new reality.

~ Dream Bit ~

Big Dreamers Live With Empathy For Others

Big Dreamers move about their days with great compassion and empathy for others.

They never forget where they came from.

It's this energy that inspires Big Dreamers with a desire to lift others up.

Listening to him speak about his parents, fills me up with love and light. He is so proud of the influence his parents had on his life. He has seen them through their rise and fall, and is on an exalted mission to help them regain prosperity. He is fulfilled with a purpose that far exceeds his own success. I truly admire the commitment of this young man and his desire to always surround his family with love.

When I asked him what he would share with his younger self, given the opportunity, I was inspired by his response. "I would tell myself, I'm meant for more and that I'm born to lead and inspire others. Keep going and know that every choice you make is leading you to a place of success," he shares. "I would reassure my younger self, that everything will be ok, and that our family will push through this pain," he adds. He paused for a moment, and shares how this question reminded him of the days he would drive from his parent's office to their country home. During the 30 minutes of driving, in the pitch black with only the moon and the stars, he would be comforted. "I could always find, a deeper sense of inner-peace, looking up at those stars. It was as if they were smiling down and reassuring me everything would be ok," he shares.

Reflecting back, he discerned all challenging times as opportunities to strengthen. He was sharpening his skills and preparing for success. The future he dreamed of creating, served as a shimmering haven that would soon unfold in the upcoming chapters of his life.

It's this kind of energy and words of encouragement that he would whisper into the ears of his younger self. "Embrace and accept these challenges Paddy, and remain open, it's only making you stronger. You will get through everything that life is throwing at you, if you just keep on going," he adds.

After his accident, Paddy was fired, following the life-changing eye surgery he underwent. "I wasn't surprised, I was always away at doctors appointments," he recounted. His younger brother came out to visit him, soon after he was let go from his job and Paddy chose to move back home with his brother. He was emotionally and financially burned out.

During the same time he decided to return home, his father had started a new franchise in the restaurant industry. Paddy decided to help his family rebuild their dream. He was committed to investing the next 5 years of himself towards helping his family get back on top and once again, be seen as pillars in the community.

It was at this point, McCracken & Sons Restaurant Group, was formed. He was now charging full steam ahead. He had an intention to build his success within the restaurant industry. He signed up for management courses in Arizona, where he then later ended up working. He was committed to driving success in his family's business. During his relocation to Arizona and rented a room from a 70 year-old lady. One dark night, while starring up at a starry sky, he asked himself, "What the hell am I doing here?" At this stage in his life, he knew at a deeper level, he was not supposed to be in Arizona! He had ventured out to California all those years ago to build a new level of success for himself, but now years later, he is in the same place he started. He experienced greater levels of discouragement for having to start all over again, while his friends in California were

Big Dreamers

building their dreams. Despite his greater intentions and his desire to help his family, Paddy had no interest in managing multiple restaurants. This was not his dream. "I had no experience running a restaurant or a bar," he recounted. Even though he was going through some emotional hurdles, he was grateful for at least earning a salary and getting back on his feet. Having a weekly pay cheque coming in was really helping him at this stage. "I felt something big was around the corner," he recounted. After three short months of running this restaurant in Arizona, a new opportunity was about to reveal itself.

He remembers the exhilaration of receiving a text from his friend in California, like it was yesterday. "I just returned from an exhausting, full day of work, but I couldn't wait to check out these opportunity videos that my friend had sent me," he shares. "I couldn't believe what I was seeing and hearing. His long time icon, someone that he respected so deeply, had just launched a new anti-aging business. Could this be possible? He thought, "Is this the opportunity I've been waiting for?" Paddy and his friends in California recognized this was the opportunity they all had been dreaming about. Similar to Paddy, some of his closer friends were also experiencing deeper challenges. He felt a kinship with all of them. He encouraged them to seize this opportunity and not hesitate a moment longer! Years of dreaming big attracted him to this one moment of clarity. Images of being at the start of the next big thing suddenly flooded his mind. He instantly saw himself, leading teams of thousands across different countries. He experienced the feeling of travelling abroad and inspiring others to dream bigger. It was only a moment, but that was all he needed, this one moment to define himself and his future success.

He already experienced a meaningful connection to the leadership in this new company. "There was no hesitation in my decision. I was ready to allocate all of my energy to this new opportunity," he shares. He was always the go to guy that successful leaders felt comfortable approaching. People naturally trusted and confided in Paddy. He was a great listener, one of the top traits that successful leaders possess. He offered his opinion when they asked for it and he maintained their confidence.

Big Dreamers

~ Dream Bit ~
Big Dreamers Act On Opportunities

Big Dreamers are crystal clear on what they want to create. When opportunities surface their clarity helps them act swiftly and without hesitation. They don't over analyze, since they are driven by a deeper connection to their own intuition.

Paddy was ready to define and create the next chapter in his life. He listened closely to what his heart and inner voice was telling him. He knew that leaders he respected were prepared to leave their successful businesses to join this new opportunity. He knew this would soon change the course of his life. He had spent the past several years when living in California cultivating deep relationships with successful leaders, so he was able to recognize the power in this opportunity. "The one man I admired, for so many years, was now coming out of retirement, to start up this new company in the anti-aging market, I was in," he recounted. Paddy didn't even question, whether it would work or if he had sufficient funds to get started. He didn't need to look for any signs to tell him what he already knew. The only sign he needed was GO! He had a credit card and he didn't worry about how he was going to pay off the start-up fee. He just knew, with every cell in his body, this was the opportunity of a lifetime and he was not prepared to let it pass him by.

When Paddy heard about it, the company was only 20 days old. That didn't seem to faze him though. This was his time to assume a key leadership role. He was ready to lead himself to the life and the success he deserved and this was the ticket for the ride of his life. He was ready to lead others and invest his years of belief and personal development into showing others how to dream bigger. All of the challenges, setbacks, failures, training and development, prepared him for this moment. He was exactly where he was destined to be. It was a brilliant unfolding from the universe, conspiring in his favour, taking him to epic levels of leadership and success. "It was a feeling of awe and joy, as if this was it," he recounted.

Personal development was the main catalyst that changed his life. All of the actions and choices he made resonated from this centre. Personal development anchored him like deep roots in a tree. The storms and winds of change, he had faced throughout the years never toppled him. It enriched and nourished him. It was his guiding light, during his darkest times. From the age of 16, he was exposed to some of the most impressive thought leaders, like Bob Proctor. It was the willingness of his parents to expose him to personal development, at a young age, that nurtured his growth. He speaks of his father, Michael, as being his hero. He had fond memories of him attending

Dale Carnegie classes and sharing his experiences with him. Books like, *Think and Grow Rich*, by Napoleon Hill and *How to Win Friends and Influence People*, by Dale Carnegie, filled the McCracken family library. It was this commitment to personal development that became a powerful force in his life.

Even though he made the leap into this new start-up company, he wasn't naive. He knew it wasn't a "get rich quick" opportunity. He continued to work 60-hour weeks at the restaurant and bar, while diligently building his new company in his spare time. "I found myself always looking outside the window and dreaming of the life and the people I wanted to surround myself with," he shares. While in the sports bar, watching championship games on the big screen, he was instantly transported back in time sitting next to his brother at major sporting events. The lifestyle he knew at a young age, included meeting athletes like Michael Jordan and sitting in courtside seats. Paddy wanted to share this lifestyle with his brother again.

Watching these sporting events at the bar, he suddenly realized he should be there, live and sitting in the front rows like he experienced as a kid. He wasn't ready to settle for a below average life. Greatness and success flowed through his veins and he was filled with a greater sense of urgency to define his life. It was as if he was following a self-fulfilling prophecy. He believed in himself and in his ability to reconnect his family to the success they knew and lived for so many years. "I never felt any negativity for the current state of our lives, I just knew that I had to get us back there," he recounted.

He was a Big Dreamer and this energy of success surged through every part of his body. He could see, feel and touch his dreams. All he had to do was close his eyes and know that success was just around the corner. Time suddenly felt like an illusion. He already tasted high levels of success and it was now just a matter of time before it became his only reality. "If I wasn't watching sports on the big screen or training my staff, then I was starring deeply out the window dreaming of the lifestyle I knew I could re-create," he recounted. He felt he could be anything, create any lifestyle and even own any restaurant if he wanted to. The Big Dreamer was now bustling and ready for epic levels of success.

He gazed at his current life, the low salary and lack of health benefits. He felt like a slave to a system that suppressed his passion for living a bigger life. He knew he and his family were meant for so much more. He accepted the reality they once were on the top of a mountain and they fell. He understood he could fail and fall, but then choose to get back up and create new levels of success. "One day, I will open my own restaurant, and take care of my staff by pouring inspiration and personal development into them," he shares. When working in the restaurant industry he was astonished as to how most employees are stifled in organizations, as if they aren't even part of the human race. All of these observations, influenced him in creating a new world, one where he could inspire a new generation of leaders.

One of the common denominators that exist with all Big Dreamers is their willingness to replace older conditioned habits with new successful ones. When I asked him what bad habits he had to replace, he confidently responded, "I had to stop spending the money

I didn't have and start taking care of the debt that was accumulating," he shared. He was ready to develop a new and responsible financial mindset. He had a long-held desire to cultivate personal leadership, which included managing his life and finances proactively and responsibly. He appreciated that successful people, didn't live their lives this way, hoping and wishing for things to improve. He had spent enough time around Big Dreamers and knew they created exactly what they focused their minds on, including managing their finances with precision. He was in a state of rebuilding his credit rating and his overall approach to financial stability. Even during these turbulent times, he set his mind and his vision on prosperity. With every passing day, he was honing his skills and gaining confidence by taking 100% responsibility for the life he believed he could create.

One of the new success habits he focused on developing, was confidence with front stage activities. Up to this point in his career, he had mastered a lot of back stage details and administrative functions. He recognized a need to hone his skills with presentation and communication. In the past, he would do whatever he could to avoid cold calls and three-way support calls (an effective sales method, by using a third party, to endorse a product or opportunity). "I would even fake getting disconnected with a prospect, just to avoid having to engage in a three-way call," he shares. He avoided these kinds of sales approaches, simply out of fear, as he didn't want to stumble or look foolish. He recognized that this kind of avoidance would not serve his higher self. He knew he had to embrace becoming comfortable with being uncomfortable, in order to thrive as a future leader.

His traditional and formal education, would not prepare him for the new skills he had to master. It was easy for Paddy to get through high school by hiding, but now, he had to learn new types of front stage leadership skills that started with thrusting himself out of his comfort zone. In order to inspire thousands of other people, he had to first lead himself and put his own oxygen mask on. "I couldn't be a leader to others, without first leading myself and taking responsibility for my life," he shares. "I couldn't ask others to do things that I was not first prepared to do myself," he adds.

He believes there are no limits to his success, happiness and fulfillment today. He is focused on re-igniting the passion and desire he felt during the first year of his new business. He has a keen interest in taking his personal relationships to whole new levels, and is ecstatic about attracting the greatest love of his life. He was in bewildered awe the moment he met her.

He presently lives in a whole new reality. He purchased his dream home and is conducting this interview from his new state-of-the-art, high tech office, something that seemed like just a dream not so long ago. He always adhered to the belief his team would be a success. "There was never any doubt in my mind, about what this team could do," he recounted. His reinvention has attracted new levels of success and love into his life. He is on a mission to inspire so many others to Dream Bigger and create the life of their dreams.

One of the first goals he wrote on his sleek, glass backboard, in his office, is to help create 100 millionaires by the year 2020. He's filled with great pride in leading one of the largest teams that organically built itself from the ground up. He shares how collectively his team self-generated close to $120 million in sales last year. "How could this happen? Well, of course it happened! I knew and believed it was possible," he shares.

His tenacity and commitment to personal development opened up a world of possibility. He continues to embrace an energy of humility within his style of leadership. While other leaders prefer to 'hype it up', he takes on a grass roots approach by strengthening his ability to communicate more effectively. His training approach is focused on generating deeper levels of memory retention within his team. Day-by-day he focuses on duplicating his efforts through learnt lessons and strives to create a ripple of confident leaders.

Paddy often dreams of a future that far exceeds the accumulation of wealth, but rather one of philanthropy and purpose. "It's what the money can do for others that means so much to me," he shares. He always perceived this opportunity, as a catalyst for others, right from the start. He looked beyond the benefits of simply representing a world-class anti-aging product. He's driven by what this global opportunity can do to change people's lives.

He reflects on a recent training event in Indianapolis that rocked him to his core. A little 8-year-old girl took the stage and shared how she got her dad back as a result of this opportunity. She went on to share how much she treasures her time with her dad. Listening to this little 8-year-old girl on stage, Paddy was instantly transported back in time to a young boy attending similar events with his parents. The positive energy and role models that surrounded him, helped chisel the young successful man he is today. The roots that so strongly support and anchor his success presently have been growing for years below the surface. "I'm surrounded by an incredible mix of individuals on my team with such a diversity of skills and tremendous qualities," he shares. "The opportunity we have going forward, is endless, so dreaming big is such a big asset for us," he adds.

His confidence, humility and desire to transfer his belief into others, puts him in a unique position to influence positive change throughout the world. "If I can be and do anything, then why can't others," he shares. Only recently has he started to embrace, and share the challenging journey his parents had to endure. He knows that falling, is only temporary and getting back up will always be a choice. Like most Big Dreamers, he's inspired to share his life lessons with others, knowing it will help them push through the pain. He's inspired that his parents have managed to stay connected and grow closer as a family unit during these demanding years. He continues to see them, as incredible role models that influence the way he will approach the start of his family.

One of the greatest things he learnt in life, is it doesn't matter how many times you fall down, inside each one of us is an ability to dream bigger and fail better. "Where there is a will, there is a way," he adds. He shares the significance and the power in developing yourself personally. He sees the opportunity to learn wisdom in every experience that we go through. Like all of his mentors before him, he believes it's the consistency and persistency in developing the little things that will move your life forward. "When you master the little things, then the big things will take care of themselves," he shares.

He wants to be remembered for being a man that was present, with everyone in his life, and never stopped developing himself. He admires highly successful people that are continually learning and growing. It is the billionaires who continually write great ideas down in their little notebooks that inspire him. "Personal development is the oxygen that can help anyone create a new mindset and belief system," he adds. His message to readers is one of action, "I want to encourage everyone to take chances, try, and do more than what you've done in the past."

~ Dream Bit ~

Big Dreamers Are Willing To Do Something New

Big Dreamers recognize that to reach new levels of success and fulfillment, they have to be willing too try something new they didn't already do.
They focus on breaking habitual patterns that don't serve their higher self.

"Failure is nothing more than feedback, which gives us the opportunity to try different things," he shares. Most people see failure as roadblocks preventing them from moving forward and embracing the opportunity to refine their approach. His much-deserved success is a result of continually observing and learning from others. Even though he doesn't recall every conversation, he remembers the feeling of these important encounters with the leaders that shaped his life. He encourages readers to lead with love and listen to their own inner voice. He wants you to develop a burning desire to change your life. He shares a profound insight to never stop loving yourself throughout the journey and the challenges. By embracing the journey and not the destination, it will bring you the success, happiness and fulfillment that your heart desires.

Paddy was always a Big Dreamer that wanted to play and win big. He always dreamed big for not only himself, but for his friends and family. This was his compass that guided his actions. He lives each breath with tremendous gratitude for the amazing people he has surrounded himself with and continues to attract. He never stopped dreaming bigger, taking action and bustling after his success. As long as his family stayed connected, he knew they would be ok. "I was so fortunate to have such a great mom, dad and brother," he shares. His family was always united in love. Reflecting back, the only regret was the years that he couldn't afford to travel home to be with them. He's so grateful that his entire family now resides in the same city. He loves experiencing a weekly family dinner, hiking or sharing something as simple as a movie together. "I never take our family time for granted," he adds.

He feels like he's just starting to live his best life. He believes with sheer humility that his bigger dreams have yet to surface. He believes his future is deeply rooted in his past upbringing and development of himself. His greatest wish for others is to seek out positive role models, that instil greater levels of belief and that they can emulate. He continues to grow himself by listening to others and lavishes in the thought of inspiring a world of Big Dreamers.

~ A Dedication from Paddy's father, Michael McCracken ~

Our children are our greatest blessing! Paddy made parenting a blessing and a joy. As working parents of a growing business he spent a lot of time with us and was surrounded by loving family, friends and business associates. All of who were incredible role models with values, morals and impeccable character. In the early years, while toddling off with us, to yet another meeting, most topics were beyond his understanding. He would be colouring, reading books or fidgeting like all little boys, yet there is no doubt he was internalizing and processing the information at some level. His knowledge, wisdom and understanding of people and business was apparent as he grew up and spent more time with us. He emulated a strong work ethic and he desired to be, and want more out of life. Continued education and life experience, broadened his vision and inspired his dreams to build and have a business of his very own one day. Every day he makes us incredibly proud, as he continues to thrive and grow as a human being, leader and mentor. We applaud his strength and courage as he experienced the hardships of life struggles, yet has never lost his vision and purpose, of becoming the best he can be and inspiring others to do the same. The greatest gift one can give is to help others see greatness in who they are and who they can truly become.

Cheerful Blessings Padraic Gerwig McCracken ~ No parents could love you more!

In this new age, you no longer need to be an expert that knows WHAT or HOW. It's far more fun to be a passionate amateur on fire with a purpose. Seek out the amateurs that don't know what the HELL they are doing, you'll find their spirit far more interesting.

~ Gerry Visca

9. Share & Tell
GET INVOLVED

"Find your voice, shout it from the rooftops, and keep doing it until the people that are looking for you find you." ~ Dan Harman

Now you too can be apart of inspiring a world of dreamers. At this point, I hope the dreamer inside of you has been stirred up! One way you can keep this dream alive is to share and inspire others around you to dream. If we are to survive and thrive as a human race, the world needs this now more than ever. Sharing your dream, these stories and this book inspire others around you. This is a world inspired, a world of 1 million Whys. So, will you help create it?

I believe it is time to create a new ROI for the world; one where we **R**each **O**ut and **I**nspire others. As you use this book to ignite and keep your dreams alive, consider posting photos and inspiring comments of you, with your copy of Big Dreamers; use the two hash tags #whyguy and #bigdreamers. You might also consider creating a Big Dreamers book club. Keep sharing the stories of this book and be inspired to share your own. Attend our book signing events and visit our official store @ defyeneurs.com/mag, to order more copies and our Defyeneurs magazine.

#whyguy #bigdreamers

Check List
IGNITE YOUR DREAM TO ACTION

- Re-read this book. Keep it with you for when you feel off track. Compliment this book with, *I Don't Know What The HELL I'm Doing!*® order @ www.gerryvisca.com/hell
- Highlight the top 3 "Dream Bits" that you're stepping into this year.
- Cultivate one success habit every month.
- Order the *GET CLEAR*© pdf worksheet by emailing gerry@redchairbranding.com
- Inspire others and take a photo of yourself holding this book; share it on social media.
- Reach out and inspire others - order a copy of this book for your workout partner @ www.defyeneurs.com/mag
- Create a monthly accountability session with your workout partner.
- Schedule Big Dreamer Book Reading Clubs once a month or use the book in training sessions.
- Fill out the Ignite your WHY© worksheet and keep it close to you.
- Update your social media profiles with *Why you Exist.*
- Schedule a 12-month launch party to celebrate your vision.
- Write out your top affirmations starting with, *I am...*
- Create a new dream board, so you can see it every morning.
- Commit to training your mind and visualizing your dream with a morning meditation. Reach out to Angela Kontgen @ angela@angelakontgen.com

Ignite your WHY
Worksheet
PASSION + PURPOSE = OUTCOME

PASSION

What excites me and makes me come alive?

_____

_____

What actions bring me the greatest joy?

_____

_____

PURPOSE

What service do I love giving away to others?

_____

_____

OUTCOME

What do I want to be remembered for?

_____

_____

_____

Scan this page to access this video training.

Visualization

Work Sheet

**Describe your ideal picture of what you want
your life to look like (WHY, WHAT, WHERE, WHEN, WHO)
Be as specific as possible.**

WHY DO YOU WANT IT?

_____

_____

_____

WHAT DO YOU WANT?

_____

_____

_____

WHERE DO YOU WANT TO BE?

_____

_____

WHO DO YOU WANT TO BE?

_____

_____

WHEN DO YOU WANT IT BY?

_____

_____

**Scan this page to access
this video training.**

Get Clear
Time Planner

Big Dreamers

Keep the energy alive by using this *GET CLEAR©* Planner. Get intentional and proactive about carving out time for your Big Dreams, even if it is only an hour each week. If you don't schedule time to create, launch and live your vision, it won't come to life. This exercise will also bring awareness to how little time you are presently allocating to your dreams. Use the weekly section, to schedule in high pay off activities. If you can, consider blocking out a specific day(s) for your Big Dreamer activities. For instance, block out "writing days", if you are an aspiring author.

The monthly section is intended to help you project the milestones you intend to reach through out the year. These milestones are targets to help you stay the course. This is a proactive design tool, intended to help you carve out the time and establish higher-level goals throughout the year. Keep it with you in a day timer and review it once a week.

The questions I've asked you along the right column are intended to help you focus your energy on what you want most, so please do your best in answering them, they will align your actions with your bigger dream.

MY GET CLEAR PLAN

CLARITY | LEGACY | ENERGY | ATTITUDE | RECEIVING

My Prioritization Schedule at a Glance:

	MON	TUES	WED	THURS	FRI
MORNING – 10:00AM					
MORNING – 12:00AM					
AFTERNOON					
EVENING EVENTS					

WHAT DO I WANT TO ACCOMPLISH MOST:

COPYRIGHT REDCHAIR™ BRANDING INC.

My Monthly Milestones at a Glance:

JAN	FEB	MAR	APR	MAY	JUNE	JULY	AUG	SEPT	OCT	NOV	DEC

WHAT DO I WANT TO ACCOMPLISH MOST:

COPYRIGHT REDCHAIR™ BRANDING INC.

Describe your success as if it has already occurred:

What do I want to create this Year?

My 5 BIGGEST goals are:

What do I want to be remembered for?

What brings me the most joy?

GERRY VISCA

Affirmation

Work Sheet

Describe your future success in all areas of your life:

Career, Family, Love, Relationships and Finances.

Read out loud these "I AM" statements everyday.

I AM _____

_____

I AM _____

_____

I AM _____

_____

I AM _____

_____

I AM _____

_____

I AM _____

_____

I AM _____

_____

I AM _____

_____

I AM _____

_____

Big Dreamers

Goal Setting

Work Sheet

List 3 concrete life and business goals to be achieved within the NEXT 90 days.

1 _____

_____

2 _____

_____

3 _____

_____

For each 90 DAY goal, list 3 NEXT-BEST actions you can take.

1 _____

_____

2 _____

_____

3 _____

_____

Scan this page to access this video training.

Personal Brand

Work Sheet

Big Dreamers

List 3 top attributes that best describes you. Ensure you focus on the core attributes that clearly differentiate you. <u>WHY</u> does it matter to others?

_____

_____

_____

_____

List the 3 images that best capture the essence of you:

_____

_____

_____

_____

Exercise your visual muscles.
Cut and paste some images that best reflect you & WHO you want to be.

#1. This reflects the REAL me

#1.

259

#2. This is who I want to be.

#2.

#3. This is how I want to be remembered.

#3.

About the Author

Gerry Visca

He's on a mission to inspire 1 million Whys. As a top inspirational speaker, a 14-time author and publisher, Gerry Visca exists to creatively inspire people and their ideas to action.

His education in architecture opened his mind to the world. He sharpened his skills as an award-winning Creative Director through Redchair Branding®. His global work with leaders and organizations across 10 countries inspired him to shift energy and focus towards creating a new ROI for the world; one where we know why we exist and Reach Out and Inspire others.

His writing is expressed daily on his blog, which he usually writes from his front porch, while enjoying a fresh cup of coffee, sitting next to Angela. The books and magazines he publishes, evolve out of a desire to inspire everyday people to do extraordinary things. He is honoured in his recent opportunity to be published in Jack Canfield's latest book, *Living the Success Principles*.

Hash Tags:

#whyguy

#bigdreamers

#defyeneurs

Email gerry@redchairbranding.com

Face Book facebook.com/gerryvisca

Twitter @ Instagram @gerryvisca

Reach out to Gerry, if you wish, he's an open book!
www.gerryvisca.com www.defyeneurs.com

You can also book Gerry Visca as your inspirational speaker through his International Speaking Bureau: **www.nsb.com**
1.800. 360. 1073